Governmental Manpower
for Tomorrow's Cities

MUNICIPAL MANPOWER COMMISSION

WILLIAM O. BAKER
EDWARD W. BARRETT
WILLIAM H. DRAPER, JR.
LUTHER GULICK
RALPH LAZARUS
ROBERT E. MERRIAM
QUIGG NEWTON
JOHN A. PERKINS
JAMES E. WEBB
JOHN J. CORSON, *Chairman*

The Commission's Staff

EMERY C. WINE
Assistant to the Chairman

ALLEN E. PRITCHARD, JR.
Staff Director, February, 1960–April 1, 1962

DON R. LARSON
Staff Director, April 1, 1962–June 30, 1962
Associate Director, May, 1960–April 1, 1962

DON W. LIEF
Staff Associate

DON T. ALLENSWORTH
Staff Associate

JEAN P. MOORE
Editorial Assistant

Governmental Manpower for Tomorrow's Cities

A Report of the Municipal Manpower Commission

McGRAW-HILL BOOK COMPANY, INC.

New York   Toronto   London

GOVERNMENTAL MANPOWER FOR TOMORROW'S CITIES

Graphics by Spear Visual Studios

Preface

The increasing failure of America's urban governments to attract and retain quality personnel has long been the deep concern of responsible civic leaders throughout the United States. The American Municipal Association, the American Society of Planning Officials, and the American Institute of Planners, recognizing the present and growing needs of this country's burgeoning population for top-flight engineers, planners, technicians and administrators, petitioned the Ford Foundation for the resources to make a thorough study of this problem.

With generous understanding, the request was granted. James E. Webb, whose long record of accomplishment in the public service is well known, was invited to organize the Municipal Manpower Commission, and to formulate plans for a study which would provide detailed guidelines to local governments in their search for trained and talented manpower.

Mr. Webb presided over the Commission's deliberations until January, 1961, at which time he was appointed Administrator of the National Aeronautics and Space Agency by President John F. Kennedy. I have been privileged to

v

succeed him and to serve with an able and experienced group of men and women in directing the Commission's work and formulating the report presented here.

My colleagues on the Commission are: William O. Baker, a distinguished scientist and Vice President of Research for the Bell Telephone Laboratories, Inc.; Edward W. Barrett, Dean of the Graduate School of Journalism of Columbia University; William H. Draper, Jr., member of the firm of Draper, Gaither and Anderson; Luther Halsey Gulick, Director of the Institute of Public Administration; Ralph Lazarus, President of Federated Department Stores; Robert E. Merriam, distinguished author and former government official; Quigg Newton, President of the University of Colorado; and John A. Perkins, President of the University of Delaware.

The ideas of many people and the experiences of many local governments have influenced the development of the Commission's report. For example, the Commission sought the advice of seven organizations specializing in governmental problems to aid it in identifying the manpower problems of urban governments:

The Massachusetts Institute of Technology–Harvard Joint Center for Urban Studies studied the future of American urban areas and the growing administrative responsibilities to be borne.

The Public Personnel Association investigated the recruitment practices of local governments.

The International City Managers' Association surveyed how and to what extent local governments train and develop their own administrative, professional, and technical personnel.

Griffenhagen-Kroeger, Incorporated, weighed the concepts underlying personnel administration in local governments.

The Public Administration Service studied the need for and possible shape of a national clearinghouse that might provide broader opportunities for local governmental personnel.

The University of Pittsburgh Graduate School of Public and International Affairs analyzed the career opportunities that exist in urban government. Excerpts of their report are presented as Appendix 2 of the Commission's report.

The American Society of Public Administration canvassed representative members of this profession to gain a peer judgment of administrative, professional, and technical personnel in local governments.

The Commission is also obligated to a number of informed people for their advice and assistance: Charles R. Adrian, Director, Continuing Education Service, Institute for Community Development and Services, Michigan State University; Orvis F. Collins, Assistant Professor of Social Research, Michigan State University; George H. Esser, Jr., Institute of Public Administration, University of North Carolina; Frederick Gutheim, President, Washington Center for Metropolitan Studies; Allen D. Manvel, Chief, Governments Division, Bureau of the Census; Wallace S. Sayre, Dean, Department of Public Law and Government, Columbia University; and Coleman Woodbury, Department of Political Science, University of Wisconsin.

Among others who were of valuable assistance to the Commission were Henry M. Bain, Jr.; Royce Hanson; W. D. Heisel; Louis J. Kroeger; Frederick C. Mosher; Harvey S. Perloff; Wendell Schaeffer; Herman M. Somers; Mary Eleanor Spear; Stephen B. Sweeney; James R. Watson; Robert W. Wilson; Robert C. Wood.

The Commission is also indebted to over 1,700 municipal executives in 125 cities, whose responses to its Urban Executive Questionnaire provided the basic facts for "A

Profile of the Municipal Executive," Appendix 1 of this report.

We are especially grateful to more than 600 local officials and civic leaders in sixty metropolitan areas who granted interviews to members of the Commission's staff in its quest for answers to the underlying problems facing local governments who seek qualified personnel.

Finally, we are indebted to many able minds that helped the Commission unravel a fascinating, sometimes alarming problem; to the Ford Foundation for its generosity; and to those who will take the time to read our findings, discuss them, and strive to bring about the conditions necessary to attract and retain able men and women to work in local government.

John J. Corson
CHAIRMAN

Contents

Governmental Manpower
for Tomorrow's Cities

1

The Problem: The Metropolitan Area

*Within the next twenty years we shall, in
all likelihood, make the decisions that will
determine eventually whether this new human habitat, the metropolitan area, will become the most expensive jungle or a place
fit to be the City of Man.*

—PETER DRUCKER

The City of Man must be built by men.

It will be shaped by leaders and followers, by politicians,
by suburbanites and by city dwellers, by the thoughtful and
the unthinking, by neglect of the apathetic.

It will be shaped by people.

There is a vital corps of people who man our urban front
lines, but who have been unduly ignored. They are the
men and women who face the growing problems of local

government day and night. It is they who perform the specialized services which go largely unnoticed by the public. They search out the facts, list and evaluate action and alternatives, advise local legislators, resolve other questions within policy directives and laws, carry out policy decisions, and then start the process all over again. These men and women are the administrative, professional and technical people without whom these governments would falter. In this report we call them the APT people, using the three initials as a convenient means of identification.

This report of the Municipal Manpower Commission is about APT people—Administrative, Professional, Technical—the chief executives, attorneys, engineers, accountants, doctors, chemists, psychiatrists, biologists, sanitarians, public safety experts, computer programmers, planners, personnel experts and others who staff our modern cities, urban counties, special districts and authorities.[1] It is about the quality of these APT people, their future roles, and what must be done to get an adequate number of qualified APT people into urban local governments.

This report is based on the first national study dedicated solely to the problem of revitalizing local governments through better use of vigorous, capable, dedicated APT people. These people work in a tangled, complex and be-

---

[1] This report is not about teachers and the administrators and specialists employed in local school systems. The quality of these people is also essential to the effectiveness of local governments. But the problems associated with the recruitment and retention of school personnel are different from those of other occupational fields, and have been dealt with in numerous other studies.

wildering environment. An understanding of that environment and the problems it poses is a prerequisite to any meaningful discussion of their role in shaping the City of Man.

METROPOLITAN GROWTH

Two-thirds of all Americans live in metropolitan areas. In the last decade, the metropolitan population increased by 29,000,000 or 35 per cent. Practically all of the country's population growth occurred in metropolitan areas.

These large-scale urban areas are essential to our national economy. An ever-larger share of the national product is produced, distributed, and consumed in them.

They are dominant in cultural and scientific life. Almost all of our symphony orchestras, museums and libraries, big league sports, as well as most of our great universities, hospitals and research centers, are located in metropolitan areas.

Metropolitan growth is a result of rapid increase of U.S. population and continued concentration of population in urban areas.

Why the increase? There are many reasons: better health and longer lives; wide-spread prosperity and larger families; and a bumper crop of post-war children growing into adulthood, getting married and having children earlier than their parents did.

Why concentrated in metropolitan areas? Opportunities are there for nearly every occupation in society, and in-

CHART 1

The United States Is Becoming Overwhelmingly Urban

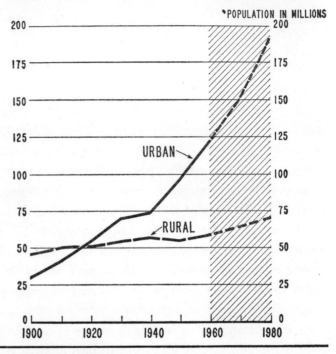

* POPULATION IN MILLIONS

URBAN POPULATION AS A PERCENTAGE OF THE TOTAL

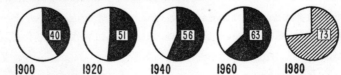

Source: (1) U.S. Bureau of the Census
(2) Philip M. Hauser, "Population Perspectives" (projections)

4

comes are higher. Metropolitan areas are magnets for both highly trained professionals, managers, scientists, teachers, and for millions of workers who provide services.

Concentration in the metropolis is not limited to a search for careers; resident and tourist alike find variety, choice, challenge and the many amenities cities add to civilization.

The change from an agrarian to an industrial economy, which has been under way since the founding of the Republic, is creating a new human environment—the metropolitan society. Technology swiftly affects metropolitan areas. Between 1940 and 1957, for example, 13,000,000 persons moved from farms to urban areas, displaced by new technologies—mechanized farming, new and better seeds and fertilizers, and modern knowledge of animal husbandry. Today only 1,500,000 farmers produce 87 per cent of America's food and fiber—enough to feed and clothe a population of 185,000,000.

Our competitive, industrial economy brings to millions of Americans an affluence, leisure, mobility and cultural opportunity that we confidently expect to grow even more in the future. Unfortunately, our thinking about local governments, despite their responsibilities for much of our daily living conditions, has stagnated. We lack a realistic expectation of what local governments should provide or cost. We also lack an appreciation of the human skills and leadership which they require. Too many people think of local governments as composed of trash collectors, police and firemen, and fail to realize the range of tasks to be done and of human talents needed.

Growth Creates Severe Problems

While the metropolis makes possible increased productivity and a richer social and cultural life, it also is the locale of many of our most severe domestic problems, including:

Social Problems. Racial tensions, juvenile delinquency, disruption of family life, mounting crime rates.

Physical Problems. Wasteful patterns of land development, lack of recreation space, slums and blighted areas, traffic congestion, water shortages.

Political Problems. Obsolete governmental machinery, fragmentation of power among hundreds of local governments, rivalry between central cities and suburbs, conflict arising from the bias of rural, small-town-dominated state legislatures, uncoordinated federal programs.

Financial Problems. Tax resources do not keep pace with rising city expenditures, tax rates soar in the suburbs, local government debts mount, taxing power of local governments is limited by state restrictions.

Many of these problems result from sheer population growth and changes in the age distribution of the population. For example, the number of Americans reaching age 18 will increase every year during the 1960's. Each new adult will require a job, space to raise a family, transportation facilities, and public services such as police and fire protection, clean water and trash collection. At the same time, people age 65 and over will number 20,000,000 by 1970, perhaps 25,000,000 by 1980. The prospects are that the average income of these elderly persons will not provide what Americans regard as life's essentials: adequate shelter, medical care, healthy diet, decent clothing.

Increased population also spurs physical growth. Each additional 1,000 persons today urbanize 100 acres; most of them settle in the metropolitan fringes. Between 1950 and 1960, the suburban population outside city boundaries grew 41 times faster than city population. This spreading urbanization has made the need for schools, for better transportation, for recreation space, acute in metropolitan areas.

While some problems result from population growth, others are the product of changes in the economic and physical structure of urban areas.

The vitality of central cities, the foundations on which metropolitan prosperity has rested, has been sapped in many areas. The hearts of many great cities are marked by spreading slums and commercial blight. Their transit systems are inadequate for today's needs and outmoded for tomorrow's. In Los Angeles, two-thirds of downtown's 3,300 acres have been turned over to the automobile for expressways, streets and parking.

Business activity as well as people has steadily moved outward from central business districts. In 1954, for example, retail sales in the ten largest metropolitan areas showed that, of the $51.4 billion in retail sales, $23 billion, or about 45 per cent, was tallied outside the hub cities of the areas.[2] In Los Angeles, Boston, Pittsburgh, and San

[2] U. S. Bureau of the Census, *County and City Data Book* (Washington, D. C.: Government Printing Office, 1957), pp. 346–359.

Francisco, central city establishments accounted for less than half the retail sales.

Into the central city, however, pour the new migrants—the displaced farmer, the Negro and the Puerto Rican.

These take the place of yesterday's immigrants from abroad. They are funnelled into the slums, or they create new slums from simple overcrowding. And because they often fail to find adequate housing, employment, education or recreation, they are the source of some of our major social problems.

Local governments have found increasing difficulty in adjusting to these changes. Central cities are asked to meet demands for expanded social services, improved traffic systems and elimination of physical blight. Suburbs, the mecca for those who seek a wholesome neighborhood in the historic American tradition, must build complete physical plants and urban service systems from scratch. Local governmental boundaries set off the rich from the poor, fragment the tax base, accentuate a sometimes serious competition, and make difficult a sense of community for the entire urban area.

The Municipal Manpower Commission is not the first to document these problems. It does not share the pessimism, currently widespread, that these problems cannot be solved. They must be solved if men are to shape the City of Man. No nation has a greater responsibility or opportunity to accomplish this than the United States.

CHART 2

Boston Population Distribution

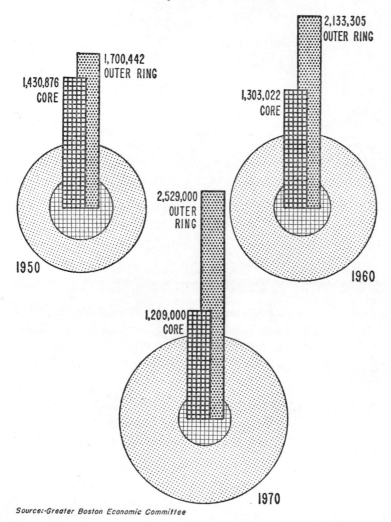

1,700,442
OUTER RING

1,430,876
CORE

1950

2,133,305
OUTER RING

1,303,022
CORE

1960

2,529,000
OUTER
RING

1,209,000
CORE

1970

Source: Greater Boston Economic Committee

We Have Seen Only the Beginning

Today's metropolitan problems are formidable, but the future will bring greater and more complex problems.

We are on the edge of America's greatest wave of urban growth. By 1980, there may be 190,000,000 Americans living in massive metropolitan areas—more than the total population of the country today.

> *By the end of the century, the United States will possess at least five super-metropolises which will have the general complexity and geographical extent of the present-day metropolitan area of New York.*
>
> —JEROME P. PICKARD

Some of this growth will take place in areas that are not yet large enough to be called "metropolitan," but most of it will take the form of growth in existing metropolitan areas. There are no foreseeable technological limits on the growth of metropolitan population and geographical expansion for the rest of the century. Advancing technology can provide enough water, power, transportation, refuse disposal and other essentials to metropolitan areas to accommodate a much larger population in a continuing pattern of low-density sprawl. Predictably, the metropolitan areas of 1980 will be much larger and more complex than those of today. Just as metropolitan areas dwarf cities, they, in turn, will be over-shadowed by more massive urban concentrations. In 1980, nearly nine out of ten Americans will

be living in urban areas, many of us in huge urban land-
scapes stretching from horizon to horizon and beyond. One
great megalopolis of perhaps 50,000,000 persons will follow the Atlantic Coast from Maine to southern Virginia.
Another will stretch from San Francisco Bay southward
through California's central valley, past Los Angeles, to
San Diego and the Mexican border.

Almost every American will feel the impact of this surge
of metropolitan growth. Today's metropolitan problems
will seem trivial within a few years. Great tracts of open
land will be overrun by bulldozers and development. The
housing and public facilities in our older cities and suburbs
will continue to age, new waves of migrants from rural
areas will pour into the cities, and millions of additional
automobiles will appear on the streets and highways.

> *Town-making will perhaps be the final
> battleground between the East and the
> West. In an affluent society, the quantita-
> tive competition is going to become less
> and less important. The final battle will
> be fought on quality.*
>
> —BRUNO ZEVI

The Bill Will Be Staggering

The costs of accelerated metropolitan growth are immense. In northern New Jersey, for example, the Regional
Plan Association estimates that to provide the essential
facilities—streets, sewers, schools, police and fire stations,
water, gas, electricity—for each new home requires an in-

vestment of $18,500. In general, the cost of the additional public services provided each year for a family approximates $1,000.

Metropolitan areas, according to estimates by experts,[3] currently require:

$600,000,000 annually to provide adequate sewage treatment facilities,

$400,000,000 annually to provide pure water,

$200,000,000 to raze one square mile of slums and rebuild it for residential purposes,

$1,250,000,000 to enable commuter railroads to maintain current levels of service.

By 1970, the annual cost of urban renewal may reach $12,000,000,000 in public funds.[4] Between now and 1980, the cost of achieving an integrated urban transportation system in the United States which would include rail, road, air and waterways may approach $100,000,000,000![5]

Experts, looking ahead to the fiscal problems of local governments, forecast increasing deficit spending, a glutted municipal bond market and fiscal starvation.

Serious as this prospect is, the Commission believes that these problems can be solved. The important question is whether the people in the city and the surrounding area understand what must be done, agree on what must be done, and are organized to act. If they are not, and we

[3] Including the Public Health Service, Professor Reginald Isaacs of Harvard University, and the American Municipal Association.

[4] Leland Hazard, "Can We Afford Our National Goals?" *Harvard Business Review*, May–June, 1962, p. 14.

[5] S. B. Zisman, planning consultant, San Antonio, Texas.

doubt that they are in many of the 212 metropolitan areas, they may in fact fall behind while thinking that they are running ahead.

When viewed by almost any convenient standard, the rapid changes resulting from metropolitan growth are not being met by policies designed to harness their impact. With another 77,000,000 metropolitan Americans expected by 1980, our problems will grow much worse before they get better.

If metropolitan growth continues so that our urban population tends to double itself ever more quickly, on a geometric rather than arithmetic basis, the problem will one day become totally unmanageable. Already, the preservation of human values, of recreation space for leisure time activities and of the cultural institutions that constitute a significant part of our modern civilization is sorely taxed by rapid growth. The prevention of crime, juvenile delinquency, mental illness and other anti-social behavior becomes more difficult as the density of population becomes greater, and as economic change and technological advances outstrip the individual's ability to adjust.

We cannot help viewing the increasingly rapid growth of our metropolitan areas with grave concern. Whether the situation will become truly acute in 1980, in 2000 or 2050, we do not know. But if present trends continue, at some time in the relatively near future in terms of history, national attention must be focused on the resulting problems.

But the picture today is not all grim. The metropolis can still be made into the City of Man. To do so, however, we must be willing to decide what we want our metropolitan areas to be, and to create the institutions through which we can achieve our objective.

LOCAL GOVERNMENT—A GROWTH INDUSTRY

Government has an all-important part to play in creating the new metropolis. While non-governmental institutions will and must do many of the things that need to be done, only government can marshal the necessary resources, exert the necessary control over human behavior, and above all, define objectives that reconcile the conflicting interests of the metropolitan area's diverse social and economic groups.

The large, rapid and insistent increase in the demand for services that plagues the local governments is an inevitable accompaniment of urban living. Urban residents depend, as never before, on governments to provide services which the individual could perform for himself in a less urban, less complex habitat; artesian wells and volunteer fire departments will not fill the needs of the metropolitan community.

Moreover, so long as we maintain our federal system, it will be the local governments—cities, counties, special districts and towns—which experience the first impact of (1) population increase, (2) migration from the farms, (3) immigration, (4) the human consequences of automation and of economic recessions, (5) increased longevity, and (6) changes in living and working patterns.

These forces make of the governments in metropolitan

areas essentially "growth industries," to use a common business term. They confront local government—as all growth industries are confronted—with the necessity of steadily expanding their capacity to meet a relentless demand for their services. Growth enterprises—governmental and business alike—require ever-increasing investment of capital, larger staffs with larger payrolls, new processes for coping with larger problems, and talented managers who can run the organization smoothly while it grows rapidly.

The managers of growth industries are constantly required to make far-reaching decisions and commitments. In metropolitan areas—and in other places where significant urban growth is taking place—key officials in government must make many such decisions. A study committee in Boston recently found this to be true.[6]

Whether the downtown business district flourishes or dies depends heavily on public decisions such as those involving tax rates, parking, urban renewal, and public transportation. Whether local industry prospers or moves often depends upon decisions as to taxes, highways, zoning, and the control of air and water pollution. Whether suburban

[6] The Greater Boston Economic Study Committee in "A Report on Downtown Boston," in May, 1959, stated: "The first step is to restore confidence in downtown Boston as a place to invest. The need is to:
1. establish tax levels and assessment practices which will encourage investment in new buildings and facilities;
2. improve public administration;
3. update building and zoning codes;
4. modernize rapid transit and automotive traffic systems; and
5. expand the scope of both public and private planning for downtown Boston and the metropolitan region."
Each of these steps involves governmental action.

developments will improve or lower the character of the metropolitan environment depends upon the foresight shown in planning for zoning, and the extension of street, water and sewer systems. Whether families will live in pleasant, attractive, neighborhoods or slums largely depends upon public decisions as to housing, density and location of schools, clinics, parks and playgrounds.

It is in the making of the decisions that are required to cope with such a burgeoning demand for products or services that the mettle of an enterprise, public or private, is tested. Foresight, imagination, skill and enterprise are required from the managers of growth enterprises. These qualities, as well as the ability to harness diverse and conflicting interests, are required of local governmental officials if they are to cope with metropolitan growth.

NO METROPOLITAN-WIDE LEADERSHIP

The future of the metropolis depends on the quality of the decisions that local governments make when confronted by such issues as these. But local governments reflect their communities. Governmental progress depends on community leadership to provide the ideas and drive needed to turn felt needs into constructive action.

The lack of area-wide civic leadership in metropolitan America has been a major cause of the failure of local governments to face up to the decisions that would accommodate growth. Without active civic leadership, political leadership will not respond to community needs. Without alert political leadership, governmental administrators lack the sustaining force of well-conceived programs.

What is the meaning of this city?
Do you huddle close together because you
love each other?
What will you answer? "We all dwell
together
To make money from each other"? or
"This is a community"?
                              —T. S. ELIOT The Rock

Edmond Bacon, a leader in the renaissance of Philadelphia and now the city's planning commissioner, puts it this way: "The future of Philadelphia will be determined, not by technological advances, but by the character of its leadership and by the strength and quality of the ideas it supports."

He adds, "A strong idea has a life of its own, and can become a dominant factor if it is clear enough, and if the leadership is stimulated to action." [7]

The impressive record made by community leadership in such cities as Philadelphia, Pittsburgh, Cincinnati, Winston-Salem, and Phoenix has confirmed Bacon's view. But in few metropolitan areas have local leaders—civic, political, administrative, from downtown and from the suburbs —banded together effectively in working out agreed upon objectives. Without such objectives, and without joint leadership and mutual cooperation, cities and their outlying

---

[7] Cited in David A. Wallace, "Renaissancemanship," *Journal of the American Institute of Planners,* August, 1960, p. 176.

areas are unable to make decisions that are sound both for the center and for the suburbs.

Why have outmoded governmental institutions persisted and why has leadership failed to lead?

The answer is clear. Our metropolitan areas—their institutions and their leaders—have been handicapped by factors which make the democratic process highly complex, and sometimes ineffective.

Mobility. The revolution in transportation and communication has hastened decentralization of the economy and has resulted in a mobile population. People constantly on the move do not develop a strong concern for their neighborhood and its future.

> *No one in this country has any roots anywhere; we don't live in America, we board here, we are like spiders that run over the surface of the water.*
>
> —VAN WYCK BROOKS

Political. The existence of some 18,000 local governments in 212 metropolitan areas makes policy formulation in these metropolitan areas an immensely difficult political and legal problem.

Economic. Older patterns of economic leadership have been challenged by the emergence of new power groups such as labor unions and racial, ethnic, and civic organizations.[8] Their devotion to specific issues results in shifting allegiances, temporary coalitions and subtle tactics. This

[8] This report does not deal in depth with labor unions in local governments. The Commission is aware of their growing importance, but

makes it difficult to attain a metropolitan-wide consensus.

Geographic. Today, many people live in one governmental jurisdiction, work in another. The residence of many leaders in suburbs removes them from the constituency which could encourage active roles in the central city.

Federal Aid. Fragmentation is further heightened by the federal system of government. More than 100 programs of grants, loans, and technical assistance to aid communities are administered by nearly 20 federal agencies. The fiscal and procurement policies and the research of other agencies also have considerable influence. Their impact has changed land use patterns, redistributed population and major industries, and reinforced the separateness of local governments. Despite these consequences, there is no significant progress toward a national urban policy.

> *The city and its suburbs are interdependent parts of a single community, bound together by the web of transportation and other public facilities and by common economic interests. Bold programs in individual jurisdictions are no longer enough. Increasingly, community development must be a cooperative venture toward the common goals of the metropolitan region as a whole.*
>
> —PRESIDENT JOHN F. KENNEDY

State Governments. The states have failed to provide leadership in the metropolitan field. Refusing to lead, they

national generalizations are difficult, if not impossible. Unions do *not* cover any sizeable portion of the APT categories; they *do* add to the dimensions of APT jobs.

have seldom aided their congeries of local governments to cope with metropolitan problems. Rather, they have retained constitutional or statutory provisions that have allowed little home rule, and little authority and revenue for local officials to use in meeting their own problems.

PERFORMANCE AND PERSONNEL

It is impossible to separate the performance of local governments from the abilities of their personnel. Ordinances are not self-executing, highways are not self-constructed, and no other service of local government has meaning except as it is planned, directed and delivered by people. If these things are done well, communities may thrive; if poorly, the future demand may outstrip all services, all facilities, all planning.

The management of local governments in the metropolitan environment is a complex activity. It requires able, skilled, experienced and mature men and women in its key positions. They must be capable of performing important responsibilities effectively, particularly in administrative, professional, and technical positions: e.g., as the heads of departments; as directors of public health clinics; as specialists in finance, traffic engineering or bridge design. Analysis by the Commission indicates that the governments in 212 metropolitan districts now employ about 230,000 such persons out of their total of 1,700,000 non-school employees. By 1980, the total will reach nearly 400,000.

In expanding their work force, local governments have

added APT persons at a rate faster than increases in total population or total employees. In Detroit, for example, between 1930 and 1960, population rose by six per cent; city employment increased by 30 per cent; APT positions jumped by about 150 per cent. As early as 1933, Leonard D. White, an authority on public administration, in discussing scientific and professional people in government, wrote that "large cities perhaps epitomize the modern reliance of government on this type of employee more completely than any other level of administration." [9]

> *Good national policies require both good organization and good people. But people are the critical factor. Wise, experienced, hard-working, incisive government officials may win out over poor organization. But poor people will defeat the best organization.*
>
> —SENATOR HENRY JACKSON

Each new activity has increased the need for capable staffing until today, a generation later, such people are even more urgently required. Persons with technical and managerial skills provide the special knowledge, background, continuity and imagination needed to keep private and public organizations abreast of new situations.

Broad Talents Are Required

In addition to more engineers, physicians, nurses, librarians and social workers, local governments employ persons

[9] Leonard D. White, *Trends in Public Administration* (New York: McGraw-Hill Book Company, Inc., 1933), p. 280.

who possess scientific training never before needed. Today, unlike a decade ago, it is not unusual to find aerial cartographers in finance departments to assist in property assessments, geologists in building inspection departments to advise on the maximum number of septic tanks that a certain type of soil can absorb, or computer programmers in traffic engineering offices to analyze the patterns of commuter traffic.

> *The final limitation on the cities' ability to make urban renewal work is an administrative one. The cities simply do not have enough competent, trained technicians and administrators to greatly increase the volume of local government activity in this crucial field.... The urban renewal administrator acts as the quarterback in a powerful backfield of politicians and civic leaders, but until he has enough specialists to block in the line, his team cannot move very much faster.*
>
> —MARTIN MILLSPAUGH

Specialists alone will not solve the metropolitan problem. To deal with declining neighborhoods, racial tensions, and political forces, men are needed who have the particular talents of the public executive. Whether elected or appointed, the public executive must recognize the needs of each group with keen perception. He must be able to lead in a public debate which formulates alternatives of significance and chooses a line of public policy. What distinguishes him most is his ability to achieve consensus at the highest possible level, with the greatest benefit to the entire community, and then to follow through with action. A city manager is an obvious example of one needing these qualifications, but today's complex issues make similar demands on department heads, and those even further down in the organization.

Administrators Face Volume

The tempo of metropolitan growth, as Harvey Perloff has written, "is hardly a situation in which the skills for handling orderly, routine tasks are to be greatly valued." The administrator of the future, according to Dean Don K. Price, will have to learn to "deal with the substance of policy," and "to organize and coordinate a complex and dynamic system to carry out policy decisions that are made by others." [10]

Roy Owsley, former consultant to the mayor of Louisville, observes that in slower-moving times there was an opportunity to investigate, debate, and weigh each issue that arose. The number and difficulty of current problems and issues, he contends, do not now permit such extended discussion, but first rate administrative minds are needed to make those decisions that must be made today and to clarify those issues that the public must decide tomorrow.

Successful administrators who direct large programs must combine public relations and political awareness with sound administrative practice and the ability to coordinate

[10] Don K. Price, "Administrative Leadership," Daedalus, Fall 1961, p. 763.

large numbers of employees representing many talents. Metropolitan administrators are finding that each dimension of their task magnifies every day.[11]

As a result of fragmentation of political units, varied sources of funds and different levels of program responsibility, APT people in local government must also be successful negotiators. They must deal with state and federal officials, with other governments in the same metropolitan area, and with private groups on many matters where the private and public sectors form a working partnership.[12]

The emphasis in administrative responsibility has already transformed higher positions in local government, from bureau and division chief upward, with a corresponding decline in purely technical responsibilities. In large cities public works directors, for example, devote only about 5 per cent of their time to strictly engineering matters. To engineering they must add administrative skills, an under-

[11] A simple example of this new complexity is the fact that the urban administrators must be able to negotiate with and make use of organized employee groups—an increasing number of them are labor unions—with quite different ground rules from those found in private enterprise. In one metropolitan authority, management is compelled to deal with 27 separate labor unions. Our larger local governments thus must have executives capable of understanding this development and its implications for local government.

[12] With responsibility for a $60,000,000 facility as well as the construction of a new $50,000,000 field to handle supersonic aircraft, Houston's director of aviation illustrates the range of APT duties:

1. He manages the facility which has grown much larger and more complicated with the development of air and ground equipment.
2. He represents the local government before state and federal agencies in regard to air routes, services, financing and regulations.
3. He negotiates with the air carriers and other concessionaires who use and lease airport facilities.

standing of the economy, and an ability to define and analyze alternative courses of action on major policy issues.

Two Obstacles Impede Governments

To secure high quality administrators, professionals and technicians, local governments face severe difficulties in times of full employment and widespread economic opportunity. There is little need to document the existence of national shortages in hundreds of occupations. At the same time, however, local governments face unique problems.

This report stresses two major obstacles which impede their efforts to attract the superior manpower they must have:

1) The working environment in metropolitan area governments, and

2) The personnel systems of local governments.

These two points emerge as most important from a critical analysis of the judgments of literally hundreds of local officials interviewed during the course of the Commission's investigations. There is widespread concern and outright fear among officials, professionals, administrators and personnel experts that the quality of APT people is too limited to administer programs which will grow larger and more complex.

We Can't Afford Second-rate Personnel

The Municipal Manpower Commission believes that the theme of excellence in the public service at the local level demands attention. A key conclusion of the Hoover Commission [13] applies to metropolitan areas as well as the national government: "We cannot entrust the government of today to second-rate men and women."

Many persons have pointed out that the competition for excellence in American society will become much more intense. Little awareness of this competition, however, or of the price of not competing, exists. Civic and political leadership has not sought far reaching revisions in the working environment.

The patronage systems of some cities and a number of urban counties are dangerous anachronisms; rigid, negative, over-protective independent Civil Service systems have also become obstacles to attracting and utilizing high caliber people. In both systems, merit is neither the goal nor the result.

> *In local governments, the executives are unable to exercise effective leadership in personnel policy and practice, the career services are overspecialized and inhospitable to new entrants at the middle or upper ranks, there is insufficient emphasis upon the talents of innovation and creativity, and there is a failure to gain recognition and high prestige for the public service.*
>
> —WALLACE SAYRE

Current personnel practices of a great many urban local governments attract moderately qualified persons at the

[13] Frank S. Endicott, "Trends in Employment of College and University Graduates in Business and Industry, 1962" (Northwestern University, 1962), p. 6.

entry level, lose the better part of this input in a few years, prevent infiltration of new blood by rigid regulations, promote from within on the basis of tenure rather than merit, thus pushing mediocre quality upward.

It is clear that this country is going to be confronted with a host of problems stemming from urban growth on a scale far surpassing anything we have known; that our governmental institutions are ill-prepared to make the necessary decisions, and to act on them; and that the development of an enlightened and energetic civic leadership on a metropolitan scale is essential to the creation of a new and better metropolis. It is similarly clear that the personnel of local governments have an all-important part to play in this process.

2

The Environment: Leaders, Institutions and Attitudes

The Municipal Manpower Commission was asked to analyze one phase of urban living: how to attract and hold able people in the service of local government. Early in our deliberations, we both narrowed and broadened that assignment.

We narrowed our vision by deciding to concentrate on the vital corps of people who lead urban government or direct the thinking about urban problems. We broadened our vision by recognizing that municipal manpower doesn't work in a vacuum. The ability to recruit Administrative, Professional and Technical—APT—municipal employees depends on a tangled web of factors; attitudes toward local government, the organization of these governments, their relationships with each other and to the states and federal government, the extent of civic interest and leadership, the financial resources allocated to local government. The Commission early recognized that some understanding of the environment and the problems it poses was an essential prerequisite to any meaningful discussion of the role of APT personnel in shaping the future of our cities.

The Commission's inquiries make clear that the challenge of metropolitan problems, and the human consequences involved, is great enough to stretch the minds and test the skills of able individuals, and to give them satisfaction. But this challenge has not been translated into attractive opportunities for the persons best-equipped, by training and experience, and motivation for public service, to deal with them.

This failure to produce opportunities results from:

1. A lack of clear community-wide objectives and of permanent machinery for area-wide planning and policy formulation.

2. Restrictive state constitutional and statutory provisions which handicap efforts by local governments to do what needs to be done.

3. Lack of coordination among federal programs that helps fragment the metropolitan community and produces conflicting results and consequences.

4. The distressingly low prestige accorded local government employees by the American citizens.

An analysis of these factors affecting the urban environment and APT personnel is necessary for a fuller understanding of the findings relating to manpower management.

The manpower findings in the following chapter stress the lack of an effective personnel system capable of recruiting, utilizing and holding able men and women.

1. *Our metropolitan areas lack clear community-wide objectives, and the leadership and institutions required for area-wide planning, policy and action.* The metropolitan area may be a unit economically but it is not politically or socially. The fragmentation of the geographical area among numerous local governments and many leadership groups is a serious barrier to the solution of metropolitan problems which are beyond the capacity of any single jurisdiction or civic organization; it is a cause of frustration for municipal manpower.

Structural Fragmentation Continues

Political fragmentation grows apace. From 1957 to 1960, 300 new units of government, mostly in metropolitan areas, were created annually on the average.[1] In 1961, some 18,-000 units—cities, towns, counties, villages, special districts and school districts—were participating in the governing of metropolitan areas—and with a high degree of independence from each other.

[1] As new governmental units are born, local government becomes less able to cope with metropolitan problems. The Sacramento, California, area has a dozen important metropolitan-wide problems; there are 208 taxing units of government within this area, no one of them possessing the scope or power to deal with any of these problems by itself. The Chicago metropolitan area has over 600 non-school units; St. Louis County has almost 100 municipalities within it. Cleveland's metropolitan area will add 90 governmental units by 1980 according to the Regional Planning Commission of Cleveland. By 1980, 45 cities, villages and townships may be added; special districts will be added at about the same rate.

Scores of governmental units, ranging from enormous central cities to minuscule suburban enclaves, from huge port authorities to special districts charged with mosquito abatement and cemeteries, make combined action difficult.[2] In the 14 largest metropolitan areas in 1950, there were 1,333 municipalities of fewer than 50,000 people. Their small size limits their ability to perform efficiently for their own citizens, and to marshal the necessary resources. A total of 8,000,000 persons depended upon these units for vital services, public facilities and planning for the future. Furthermore, the small-scale problems faced by such units do not offer much attraction to experienced and able personnel. Nor are their staffs large enough to offer careers attractive to young persons of great potential.

Most of the few efforts so far made to overcome smallness by devising metropolitan units have failed at the polls.[3]

[2] Residents of Park Forest, a Chicago suburb, in recent years have been directly concerned with the following local government entities: Cook County, Will County, Cook County Forest Preserve District; village of Park Forest, Rich Township; Bloom Township; Monee Township; Suburban Tuberculosis Sanitarium District; Bloom Township Sanitary District; Non-High-School District 216; Non-High-School District 213; Rich Township High School District 227; Elementary School District 163; South Cook County Mosquito Abatement District. (Advisory Commission on Intergovernmental Relations, *Governmental Structure, Organization and Planning in Metropolitan Areas*, 1961, p. 21.)

[3] In Cuyahoga County, Ohio, voters within the city of Cleveland and in the rest of the county rejected a charter to give the county certain area-wide powers. In St. Louis, city and suburban voters rejected a proposal to make a multi-functional metropolitan district government in the St. Louis area. In the same year, 1959, voters of Toledo and Lucas County voted against a county home rule charter which would have established the county as a municipal corporation and broadened its authority. As discussed in Conference on Metropolitan Area Problems, *Metropolitan Area Problems*, January–February, 1962, p. 3, and November–December, 1959, p. 1.

CHART 3

Metropolitan Areas Contain a Multitude of Local Governments

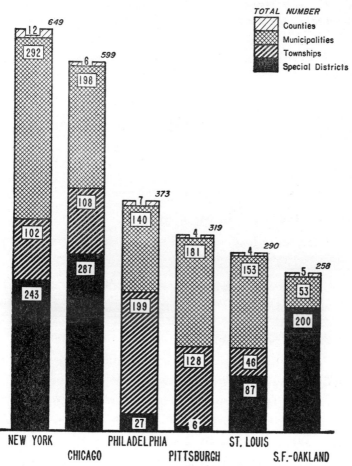

TOTAL NUMBER
Counties
Municipalities
Townships
Special Districts

649

12
292
102
243

NEW YORK

599

6
198
108
287

CHICAGO

373

7
140
199
27

PHILADELPHIA

319

4
181
128
6

PITTSBURGH

290

4
153
46
87

ST. LOUIS

258

5
53
200

S.F.-OAKLAND

Source: Census of Governments, 1957

33

Some observers see these defeats, and the continuing difficulties of the Dade County, Florida, metropolitan government, as signs that a hostile public will never accept metropolitan governments. If carefully analyzed, these failures appear to be less due to public attitudes on metropolitan government than to the resistance of local government officials to change, the failure of leaders to lead, or the resulting apathy of citizens.

Although metropolitan reorganization is a logical thing, we will never do it.

–MMC Staff field interview
Philadelphia, Pa.
August, 1961

Leaders Lead in Different Directions

Community leadership, in most urban centers, does not provide effective community-wide guidance. Division and conflict among businessmen, professional men, educators, labor union executives, and other civic leaders within metropolitan areas have made it difficult to secure area-wide agreement on metropolitan policy.

"The forces of leadership are definitely divided," a local businessman in Denver stated. "The Chamber of Commerce now represents a wide variety of interests on which they find it difficult to be effective and in agreement." A newspaper executive in Tulsa reported that "Up until a few years ago a half dozen men ran this city. Today the list would have to be much larger, and it would also have to include leaders of at least 32 separate civic groups." A

Chamber of Commerce official in Los Angeles testified that "There is no real community of interest in the business community, particularly on local government matters." In Fort Worth, San Francisco and other cities, observers reported similar diversity of economic interests and failure to achieve that consensus which is necessary for realistic community goals.

The individual civic leader, in fact, now often finds himself in conflicting roles, as his interest in the downtown business district vies with his interest in the suburb where he lives.

Goals Are Unclear

Consequently there are few communities where metropolitan-wide goals have been set and programs formulated. Successful attempts at mobilizing leadership in Cincinnati, Pittsburgh, St. Louis and Philadelphia have, it is important to note, been supported by adequate research and staff assistance. They have resulted in the attraction of able officials, the improvement of governmental services and the more effective functioning of exciting governmental machinery.

The necessary governmental machinery must provide a base for leadership, a forum for public debate on the objectives of the metropolitan community, and the means to follow through on metropolitan programs,[4] so that APT personnel will have a clear notion what the public wants.

[4] Robert C. Wood, *Metropolis against Itself* (New York: Committee for Economic Development, March, 1959), p. 37.

Without such guidance their actions today necessarily reflect timidity, lack of imagination, or surrender to those partisan groups or local communities which "make the most noise."

Planning can be a means to bring about community goals and decisions. It can educate the public and suggest solutions. Despite these advantages, in 1962 only 35 states had legislation which permitted the creation of regional planning agencies; the other 15 states contain 43 metropolitan areas which have no legal power to create such an agency; taken in total, "less than half of our metropolitan areas are served by such an agency." [5] Even with federal funds available for metropolitan planning, few areas have achieved a truly comprehensive planning program.

Before viable governments will be developed for metropolitan areas, voters and elected and appointed government officials and leaders must recognize that planning for the future is not regimentation, and that metropolitan government is not the same as super-government or the end of grass-roots democracy and home rule.[6]

Agreements Require Machinery

Conflict and controversy are to be expected in a dynamic urban area. One of local government's most critical jobs is to gain sufficient agreement on community goals, in an

[5] George Deming, "Comments" in The Advisory Commission on Intergovernmental Relations report "Government in Metropolitan Areas," Washington: Government Printing Office, 1962, p. 15.

[6] Governmental Affairs Foundation, Inc., *Metropolitan Surveys: A Digest* (Chicago: Public Administration Service, 1958), p. 21.

atmosphere of conflict and competition, to permit effective action. There is need for political machinery to gain agreement on policies for the entire metropolitan area. There is also a need for able executives skilled in formulating meaningful alternatives and, after full debate and democratic consultation, acting boldly on the agreed objectives. Neither the machinery nor the executives exist in most metropolitan areas today.

The lack of both plans and machinery has cost the metropolitan community dearly: in public funds, in natural and human resources. By hampering the development of effective solutions to problems which are too great for a single unit, these lacks have steeped high the frustrations for APT personnel who desire to solve public problems. Without the chance to exercise their fullest abilities, APT people will continue to regard local government as too sterile an environment in which to work.

2. *State constitutions, laws and procedures limit local government's ability to act to solve urban problems.* Local governments are creatures of states. Over the years, the states have imposed a fantastic variety of constitutional and statutory restrictions on local government, partly because of incompetence and corruption at the local level, partly because of traditional rural-urban antipathy, and partly because of local civic fears of extravagant practices in government.

Historically much of this state neglect of urban areas has been attributed to the fact that our state constitutions and laws were formulated in a rural era, by rural people.

As urban growth gained momentum, the rural residents' fear of city power and politics has grown, and has shown itself most clearly in the tenacity of rural control over state legislatures. Basically, this has been accomplished by the refusal of the legislatures to reapportion seats to reflect urban population increases.[7]

The concept of "home rule," where it exists, represented an effort to give greater freedom to local governments. But this concept of "home rule" simultaneously enabled the local governments to resist adjustments that would have facilitated the meeting of metropolitan problems. In many situations home rule has prevented the outward adjustment of city boundaries and has complicated the creation of metropolitan-wide machinery to cope with metropolitan problems.

State restrictions on tax sources, tax rates, local government debt, and flexibility of governmental organization are part of the governmental history of virtually every state of the union.

But no government can act without the power to act. From the point of view of 1962, from the point of view of an urban society, local governments are being asked to meet complex problems of metropolitan areas with little more power than they had to meet the needs of a rural society a century ago.

---

[7] The U. S. Supreme Court, in Baker v. Carr, 82 S. Ct., 691, decided March 26, 1962, held that the federal courts could take jurisdiction in state reapportionment cases. The rapidity with which legal actions have been filed since the Baker decision attests to the importance urban voters attach to fairer representation in state legislatures.

The governmental impacts of our urban society fall first on local governments. Logically, then, local governments should have the flexibility to meet needs and situations as they arise. Instead, the picture is characterized by limits and restrictions which take a number of forms.

Most local governments, whatever the wealth of the community they serve, are forced to rely on the relatively inflexible property tax as their major source of revenue, and must frequently live within unrealistically low property tax rates or go hat-in-hand for approval of the electorate to levy additional taxes for essential services. Everyone will acknowledge that a ten mill property tax levy cannot support municipal services, but in Ohio's local governments, voter approval is necessary to levy a higher rate. In the 57 municipalities of one county, every unit has been forced to go to the voters for increases.[8] This is not to say that states should not define the rational limits of local discretion. They do not, however, recognize the realities of 1962.

City relationships with the state are bad largely as a result of the rural domination of the legislature, particularly the Senate. There is no appreciation in the legislature for what the cities want and need.

—MMC Staff field interview, Detroit, Mich., June, 1961

---

[8] Seymour Sacks and William F. Hellmuth, Jr., *Financing Government in a Metropolitan Area: The Cleveland Experience* (Glencoe, Ill.: The Free Press of Glencoe, Inc., 1961), pp. 138, 209.

Limits placed on local government debt may have been logical several decades ago, but are the barrier to sound and prudent government today. All but 16 of the 50 state constitutions specify limitations as to the debt local governments may incur in relation to the property tax base.[9]

Many cities still lack financial strength to undertake essential services or activities because of state discrimination in allocating funds. In the distribution of state funds, large cities are consistently discriminated against. While counties receive 38 per cent of their revenue from outside sources, primarily the state government, cities receive only 14 per cent. The larger the city, the smaller its share within this average.[10] Too often this distribution in practice meets the basic needs of the county fairly, but falls far short of meeting the city's needs. The discrimination against the cities goes far beyond the contribution that they might reasonably be expected to make to governmental services in the less wealthy rural areas.

Efforts to cope with metropolitan problems, by annexation, reorganization of government, or intergovernmental cooperation, are often severely impeded by states. Few states permit municipalities to annex adjacent urbanized

[9] Indiana restricts counties to two per cent of the tax base and New Hampshire restricts its municipalities to one and three-fourths per cent. School districts in Indiana are authorized two per cent and Minnesota limits its school districts to seven and one-half per cent.

[10] The American Assembly: *The Forty-eight States: Their Tasks as Policy-makers and Administrators* (New York: 1955), p. 22, and U. S. Bureau of the Census, *U. S. Census of Governments,* "Government Expenditures and Revenues in 1956," as cited in Robert C. Wood, *Metropolis against Itself* (New York: Committee for Economic Development, 1959), p. 28.

territory without a favorable vote of the area to be annexed. As a result, a minority of voters in the metropolitan area may veto action which is essential for improved governmental service, as well as better development of the entire urban area.[11] On the other hand, incorporation is often quite easy, and is used by residents of areas outside large cities to escape, partly or completely, from the jurisdiction of the two governmental units which come closest to being metropolitan in scope—the central city and the county.

Of particular importance from a manpower standpoint are the obstacles to local governmental reorganization. Difficult-to-amend constitutions most often prescribe in detail the organization of the county and thus make almost impossible the reorganization needed to help the county cope directly with urban problems. Another form of metropolitan organization, the multi-purpose district, is extremely difficult to establish in most states.

> *Cities are too hemmed in by checks and balances to make it possible effectively to deal with the types of problems which now confront cities. These have reached the point where it is terribly frustrating for even the best people to try to get anything done.*
>
> —MMC Staff field interview, Boston, Mass. September, 1961

[11] Charlton F. Chute, "New Constitutions for a New Era in State Government," *Major Problems in State Constitutional Revision* (Chicago: Public Administration Service, 1960), p. 278.

Few states have constitutional and legislative provisions encouraging cooperation among local governmental units within a single metropolitan area. Some states actively discourage metropolitan-wide action by allocating state funds to localities in a manner that encourages the proliferation of small units. Some state constitutions also make it difficult or impossible for local officials to join in inter-local or federal-state bodies.

Thanks to this series of frequently observed impediments to the effective functioning of local governments, many local officials understandably become discouraged. Inadequate authority, poor structures and limited financial resources time and again prevent prompt action at the local level.

3. *Uncoordinated federal programs tend to fragment local programs.* The federal government does much to help meet metropolitan needs. It makes grants and loans to state and local governments, guarantees and insures mortgages, and provides research and technical assistance. About 20 federal agencies administer a large variety of programs of grants, loans, and technical assistance which affect the future of metropolitan areas. While the federal contribution is important, it suffers from lack of coordination.

The staff interviews of local government officials revealed no evidence of coordination of federal grant programs either among governmental units within the same metropolitan area or within a given unit. Federal agencies work almost exclusively with their functional counterparts on the state and local level. Little contact is made with chief executives, grants are made to functional agencies, and program cooperation between units is not sufficiently encouraged.

As early as 1955, a study of federal-state-local relations showed that "federal grants-in-aid lack cohesion and consistency because almost all of the 40 grants were created separately, are being administered separately, and are appropriated for separately, whether or not they are related programs or could be better administered collectively." [12] This lack of coordination has persisted and complicates the tasks of key executives in metropolitan areas, whose responsibility it is to see that plans for highway construction, urban renewal and housing, for example, are intimately interdependent.[13]

Not only is there a lack of coordination between federal programs, but even a single program seldom inspires combined action by all of the governments of a metropolitan area. For instance, communities within metropolitan areas do not have the authority to pool federal grants for construction of joint sewage treatment facilities or sewage

[12] Commission on Intergovernmental Relations, An Advisory Committee Report on Local Government (Washington, D.C., June, 1955), p. 38.

[13] A recent study has noted the "fragmented and conflicting impacts at state and local level of disparate federal programs concerning urban highways, urban renewal, housing, airport and sewage facilities, and construction," and proposed that: "steps be taken within both the executive and legislative branches of the national government to bring together in better coordination and inter-relationship the various federal programs which impact upon orderly planning and development within the large urban areas." The Advisory Committee on Intergovernmental Relations, *Governmental Structure, Organization, Planning and Metropolitan Areas*, July, 1961, p. 52.

lines. This situation encourages the creation of new local governmental units to provide this function.

Uncoordinated federal programs also have a serious effect on the ability of responsible local officials to make and carry out policy. Federal grants, appropriated to functional departments and agencies of the state and local level, have encouraged or even created independent and in many cases clearly autonomous administration of many programs. For example, housing and urban renewal functions are often handled by independent agencies or authorities, and are poorly coordinated with related activities of city, county or metropolitan areas.

Specialists on the local level administering federally aided programs tend to relate themselves more closely to regional and national offices of a federal agency than to other departments of the local government or other local governments within the metropolitan area.[14]

The federal government, in sum, has not tailored the administration of its grant-in-aid programs to help integrate all local government within the metropolitan area or to reinforce the capability of local government executives to manage their governments in collaboration with the executives of other local governments.

4. *Low prestige of government employment adversely*

---

[14] "Specialists have tended to build up proprietary and 'professional' interests in their own functions with administrative loyalties running vertically rather than remaining with their own level of government. For example, county and state public or social welfare workers sometimes have stronger loyalties running vertically than horizontally." The Advisory Committee on Local Government, op. cit., p. 21.

affects the quality of local government personnel. Government employment has traditionally ranked low in prestige in America.[15] It still does.

Well over half of the local business leaders interviewed by the Commission's staff indicated a negative-to-indifferent feeling toward local government and its employees. For example, the executive director of a Texas city's downtown business group stated, "The business community and citizenry don't like city government generally." A Tulsa publisher said, "This city was built completely by private enterprise and the men who built it were too proud to accept government help. We aren't sure we want the government to stick its nose into everything." A business leader in a southwestern city said a person who works for the city is a "dead-beat—a failure in civilian life."

> *I'm deeply interested in my city, but I wouldn't run for a city office for a million dollars.*
>
> —MMC Staff field interview
> Denver, Colorado
> October, 1961

[15] "Public service—whether federal, state or local—seldom evokes admiration, and attitudes toward employees working in public service run the gamut from complete indifference to hostility and contempt." (Harry Seligson, "Bureaucracy in Big Business," *Good Government*, September–October, 1957), p. 41. Also, see studies by Leonard D. White, *The Prestige Value of Public Employment* (Chicago: University of Chicago Press, 1929), and *Further Contributions to the Prestige Value of Public Employment* (Chicago: University of Chicago Press, 1932). Also see Morris Janowitz and Deil Wright, "The Prestige Value of Public Employment: 1929 and 1954," *Public Administration Review* (Winter, 1956), pp. 15–21.

The prevailing low prestige seriously limits the quality of personnel the local governments can attract and hold. Nearly half of the responses to a survey of local officials conducted by the Public Personnel Association said that low prestige was a major obstacle to recruiting persons to fill key positions in local governments.[16]

A still more striking manifestation of the effect of this low prestige of employment in local governments is found in the attitudes of municipal executives themselves. The Commission's study of 1,700 local executives revealed that only 17 per cent would recommend a career in local government.[17]

Local officials voiced strong complaints about public attitudes. They charged that educators in high schools, colleges and professional schools—in their teaching of government and in their vocational guidance—actively discourage able students from entering local government service. Furthermore, all students gain a biased view from stereotyped textbook discussions which convey an obsolete picture of the tasks, the nature of the organization and personnel of local governments.

Environment Affects APT Personnel Adversely

In all too many cases, the environment of local government offers present officials and prospective employees more frustration than challenge. APT personnel, eager to make

---

[16] In a survey of its members—professional public servants in federal, state and local governments, in universities and research bureaus—the American Society for Public Administration found that nearly half held similar opinions.

[17] For details see Appendix 1, Profile of the Municipal Executive, Part IV, pp. 163–4.

full use of their skills and energies, are forced to work without clear objectives or plans, are hobbled by an inadequate structure of local government, are confronted by other units of government that are hostile or working at cross purposes, and find that the public holds them in low esteem or is indifferent to their efforts. Under such conditions they feel a frustration that will inevitably affect the quality of their work or will drive them from local government employment altogether.

The more able personnel cannot make full use of their talents. The less able, and those who are compelled to stay by personal circumstances (such as investment in a municipal retirement system), give less to the job than they could if they were better supported by their working environment.

In a more favorable environment, quality personnel are attracted by the opportunity to prove themselves.

Impressive evidence of the importance of the working environment came from metropolitan Dade County, where the new form of government has opened new opportunities for APT personnel. A young division head remarked: "What I feel is attractive to professional government executives, in a region such as Miami, is the fact that it has recognized that services reach beyond the traditional accepted boundaries. This offers the opportunity for accomplishment on what you might call a new horizon of local government."

On the other hand, many of the government officials who were interviewed emphasized the frustrations of their work. Boston's Development Administrator stated that "cities are too hemmed in by checks and balances to make it possible to deal effectively with the types of problems which now confront cities. These have developed as the result of size and a lack of confidence in the public sector and have now reached the point where it is terribly frustrating for even the best people to try to get anything done."

CHART 4

Municipal Executives Recommend Business Careers

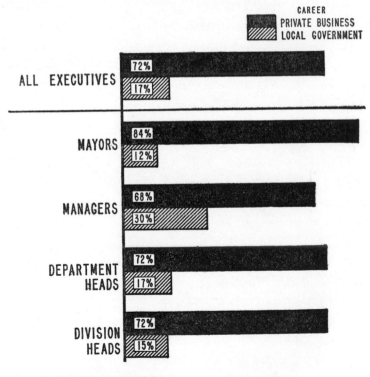

Source: Municipal Manpower Commission

> *The metropolitan form provided an added attraction, and helped make it possible to bring in a high caliber staff. When openings were announced in 1959, there were 125 applications.*
>
> –MMC Staff field interview
> Dade County, Florida
> August, 1961

It is not surprising that local government's attractions for APT personnel are inadequate to attract and hold enough of the best. There are few opportunities as challenging as metropolitan Dade County, and too many situations in which governmental structure, public attitudes, and lack of resources conspire to prevent them from doing the job demanded by their professional standards and their personal motivations.

> *I can conceive of a plan for the entire area based on a metropolitan approach to air pollution, but without the engineering and other manpower to carry it out my efforts are really frustrated.*
>
> –MMC Staff field interview
> Philadelphia, Pennsylvania
> August, 1961

Able and ambitious people do not go to work for organizations that are failing to perform the functions the public has a right to expect of them. On the other hand, a "growth industry" that is really coming to grips with its metropolitan problems can and will attract competent APT personnel.

3

The Facts: The Manpower Picture

The Municipal Manpower Commission was established "to study both the specialized personnel needs created by rapid urban growth, and the training and personnel systems necessary to attract and hold adequate numbers of competent people in managerial, technical, scientific and other specialized positions."

To carry out this assignment, to marshal the necessary facts and viewpoints, the Commission undertook the first national study focused on the people who staff and direct local governments in America's urban communities. It devoted two years to extensive research using three complementary approaches.

First, it contracted with seven organizations familiar with governmental problems to direct the minds and energies of their skilled staffs at different aspects of personnel requirements, practices and concepts.

The Massachusetts Institute of Technology–Harvard Joint Center for Urban Studies studied the impact of technology and population growth on American urban areas and the growing administrative responsibilities to be borne.

Griffenhagen-Kroeger, Incorporated, weighed the concepts underlying personnel administration in local units.

The Public Personnel Association investigated the recruitment practices of local governments.

The International City Managers Association surveyed how, and to what extent, local governments train and develop APT personnel.

The Public Administration Service studied the possible need for and design of a national clearinghouse to serve local governmental personnel.

The University of Pittsburgh Graduate School of Public and International Affairs analyzed career opportunities in urban governments.

The American Society of Public Administration canvassed representative members of this profession to gain an assessment of APT personnel in local governments.

Second, The Commission's staff concentrated on the men and women themselves who have the responsibility to make our local governments run. They accumulated details of the personal backgrounds, the experience, training and job attitudes of over 1,700 municipal executives. They sat across the desks from more than 600 local officials

and civic leaders in 60 metropolitan areas, and learned at
first-hand the facts about manpower and personnel practices. In total, the staff accumulated information concerning personnel in 221 cities with populations greater than
50,000.

Third, a number of highly capable, experienced consultants were engaged to consider the implications of the
large volume of data and opinion which were gathered.
They evaluated this material in light of their professional
backgrounds and academic disciplines and helped indicate
the most significant results of the investigations.

All three approaches centered upon the demand by local
governments for *administrative, professional* and *technical*
(APT) manpower—not rank and file manual, clerical and
stenographic personnel—and the supply available to these
units.

1. This nation needs more administrators, professionals,
and technicians than it now produces—not only to meet
the burgeoning demands of local governments but of all
public and private enterprises.

2. The prevailing philosophy of personnel administration in most local governments is not based on the need for
an adequate share of this scarce and vital talent.

3. The selection, hiring, promotion, and disciplining of
personnel, fundamental elements of management in any
enterprise, are in too many local governments, artificially
separated from, and independent of, the chief executive.

4. The personnel practices—recruitment, compensation,
and career development—of local governments are unequal

to the task of getting and keeping the number and caliber of APT personnel required.

5. There are able, competent, and dedicated persons in key positions in local government—but not nearly enough. The quality of APT personnel is, by and large, inadequate to cope with present and emerging metropolitan problems.

These five findings are distilled from a vast amount of evidence and opinion amassed by the Commission. The evidence and opinion on which each conclusion is founded are presented in subsequent paragraphs.

1. *Serious national shortages of APT personnel are rapidly intensified by growing demand for such manpower and by the inadequacy of educational programs to meet present and future needs.* The United States graphically illustrates a truth about nations: those which move ahead have immense appetites for knowledge and personal ability. This calls for an ever-larger number of highly qualified, capable people, who can keep a society up-to-date in basic theory and applications of knowledge.

Although unemployment remains an unsolved problem, administrative, professional and technical people have not been affected significantly for years. Furthermore, the range of job opportunities for today's college graduates has never been greater.[1] In this nation's continuing role as world leader—political as well as industrial—this situation must prevail.

[1] Cf. *U. S. News & World Report,* May 21, 1962, pp. 76–78.

There Are Serious Shortages of APT Personnel

The nation needs now more administrative, professional and technical persons than it produces. These shortages will intensify: between 1960 and 1970, the demand for professional and technical persons will increase 40 per cent, and job opportunities for executives and managers will also open up rapidly.[2]

This country's local governments will face much stiffer competition for talent than they did in the 1930's. At that time, they could select from the best college graduates and experienced specialists who were jobless. In the 1960's the demand for APT persons will be further heightened because the important segment of the male work force aged 25 to 44 will increase by only four per cent. This is the age range for entry and career development for most APT personnel in local government.

The shortage of engineers illustrates the national problem as it affects local governments. Currently, the nation produces about 24,000 fewer engineering graduates than the minimum needed.[3] Engineering enrollments are declining despite larger freshman classes. Most important is the fact that engineering schools produce a smaller proportion of graduates in civil, hydraulics, power and sani-

[2] U. S. Department of Labor, *Manpower: Challenge of the 1960's* (Washington, D.C., 1960), p. 11.

[3] National Science Foundation, *The Long-range Demand for Scientific and Technical Personnel: A Methodological Study* (Washington, D.C.: Government Printing Office, 1961), p. 33.

tary engineering—professional skills especially needed by urban governments.

Consider, for example, the demand for and supply of sanitary engineers. In 1958, 51 advanced degrees and four bachelor's degrees were granted in sanitary engineering. This is less than one per cent of the 5,536 sanitary engineers holding professional positions at that time.[4] Furthermore, local governments have not attracted men with advanced training. Only two department or division heads in 23 cities over 250,000 possess graduate degrees in this field.

Among the serious shortage fields are graduate civil engineers, and graduate architects. The latter are absolutely unavailable to city governments. The city ran an ad in the professional journal, overstressed good pay, and did not mention the city's name. One reply was received. When the applicant discovered this was city employment, he withdrew his application.

–MMC Staff field interview,
Cleveland, Ohio, June, 1961

A serious situation exists in traffic engineering. Among the nation's 1,500 traffic engineers, only one-third meet the professional standards of the Institute of Traffic Engineers. The annual openings number 200; the supply is about 50.

In 1958, over 2,500 key positions in state and local public health departments were vacant because not enough

[4] Donald C. Stone and Chris Heidenreich, *University Curriculums: Educational Needs for Housing and Urban Affairs* (Washington, D.C.: Housing and Home Finance Agency, 1960), p. 27.

trained persons were available. In many instances, these positions are filled either on a part-time basis, or by persons without adequate training.

New Specialties Increase Needs for Specialized Talents

Technological, social and economic changes, as well as new administrative techniques, are rapidly altering manpower needs. More people with special training are essential.[5]

The greater requirements of local governments for specialized talents have paralleled those of industry. About one in ten employees of larger cities is classified as technical, administrative or professional—about the same ratio as found in private enterprise by the Department of Labor surveys.[6] This total will rise rapidly and APT positions in local units will exceed 400,000 by 1980—an increase of nearly 67 per cent over 1960.

To the more standard list of technicians already needed in urban governmental staffs must be added an ever expanding corps of new experts to handle new functions and

[5] Ninety governments reported that their needs for ten selected specialties would increase by 1970 from 22 per cent (building inspectors) to 44 per cent (personnel technicians). The average increase was about 35 per cent. The Public Personnel Association, which made the survey, also revealed that 309 municipalities over 50,000 in population saw the need for 12,600 more positions in these ten specialties. This number must be considered a minimum, because most local governments do not project future manpower needs. For a broader view, see Appendix 2, "Careers in the Rebuilding and Management of Cities."

[6] U. S. Department of Labor, Bureau of Labor Statistics, *National Survey of Professional, Administrative, Technical and Clerical Pay* (Washington, D.C., Winter, 1961), pp. 1, 25.

processes.[7] The application of electronic computers is proceeding rapidly in finance departments, in traffic engineering, and in planning. Many units report need for qualified programmers, statisticians and other technicians. Social scientists are important to welfare, recreation, planning and urban renewal. In housing, for example, a variety of jobs has evolved since the Housing Act of 1949.[8] Specialists in relocation, housing codes, rehabilitation, and real estate are essential in active housing programs.

A state agency reports that, within ten years, specialists in sociology will be needed in public health (medical sociologists), planning (educational sociologists), parks and recreation (social ecologists). These are specialties which are almost unknown in local government.

Other specialists who have become fixtures in local units are radiation technicians and air pollution experts. The scope of their responsibilities in fire departments and public health programs increases at an accelerating pace.

Educational Programs Are Inadequate

The American society is clearly not supplying, and offers no promise of supplying in this decade, an adequate num-

[7] For a list of typical specialists in local government see Appendix 2, Careers in the Rebuilding and Management of Cities.

[8] Officials of the Urban Renewal Administration indicate that "The real limiting factor in urban renewal is not money, but manpower." Planners, real estate experts, transportation experts, urban economists, and mathematician-planners are regarded as future needs on both the federal and local levels. This will not be limited to larger units; in Ohio, for example, from 25 to 50 cities under 50,000 are planning urban renewal programs.

ber of able young people trained for the specific tasks of local government.

The reasons may be clear—a frustrating, handicapping environment within which to work; personnel administration processes that do not seek out, stimulate and utilize qualified personnel; and a public image that deprecates both the role and the worth of the local government employee.

The colleges should take a different approach to the problem of training administrative generalists and convince more students that they do not have to be Managers, but can be Finance Directors or Personnel Directors. In any case, the great deficiency of college trained people coming into urban government is in political training.

–MMC Staff field interview,
Des Moines, Iowa, June, 1961

Educational institutions and organizations for the most part do not recognize the social need for a better understanding of the problems and challenges of metropolitan areas. Very little research has been conducted in the complex area of metropolitan development to provide a base on which to build programs of education. The courses in urban economics, urban sociology and local government, offered in too few universities, are generally not functionally or operationally oriented.

The schools and colleges are failing to equip young men

and women for careers in the specialized fields of local government. A few institutions strive to meet this need, but their number is small and the total supply they generate is pitifully inadequate for the present and future needs.

Illustrations are many. There will be 3,000 vacancies each year for trained recreation workers, for example, according to National Recreation Association estimates. To fill these positions, only 600 persons are graduated annually from university programs in recreation.

There are more than two vacancies for each graduate of university city management programs; in planning there will be a need for 300 to 400 additional planners each year during the 1960's.

In summary, it is clear that demand continues to outstrip supply for many groups and, especially for those which require specific training for local governmental careers, the gap is fast growing.

2. *The prevailing philosophy of personnel administration is not aimed at getting and keeping able, well trained men and women in local governments.* Despite their growing responsibilities, political and administrative executives in local government are not supported by personnel systems aimed at providing personnel of superior ability. On the contrary, the personnel systems that exist in a great many local governments are organized and motivated by the desire to prevent political favoritism and to provide a high degree of security.[9] Their policies are founded on

[9] "The concepts of personnel administration . . . are still conditioned

two assumptions which were once valid, but which have tended to obscure the main purpose of the personnel process, which is to further the public interest through a capable public service.

Instead, the assumption is held that rigid safeguards are necessary to prevent government executives from making appointments and promotions on the basis of politics or personal favoritism.

This was true in the days when urban political organizations universally depended upon a corps of ward and precinct workers, for whom jobs had to be provided. But the character of local politics in many cities has changed sufficiently to enable many public officials to concern themselves more with getting capable employees who will help them to make a good record in office, than with rewarding their political followers.

Experience in a number of cities has demonstrated that the rigid rules and procedures of negative personnel administration can be replaced by more liberal processes without resulting in a return to patronage or spoils.

There are many interpretations of patronage and spoils. As used here, they designate the practice of basing appointments to public office on political considerations rather than on the competence and suitability of the individual for the post to be filled.

"Patronage" is usually defined as the making of appoint-

mainly by the political reform which created the merit systems, and the protective features born of the depression," reported Griffenhagen-Kroeger, Inc., to the Commission.

ments to public office to achieve political advantage or to pay a political debt; the usual implication is that little or no attention is paid to the appointee's qualification. "Spoils" usually designates an extreme of this practice. This repugnant practice directly violates the standards of quality so desperately needed in local government today. These practices are more reprehensible because they are so out-of-date—we *know* better.

> *The spoils system is not going to return. Educational standards of the people have been raised, types of campaigns for office are different than previously and need less in the way of patronage-type workers, and people do not develop the personal attachment to a candidate which requires that a candidate appoint them to a political office immediately after a successful election campaign.*
>
> —MMC Staff field interview, Quincy, Mass., June, 1961

It must be made clear that the appointment of top policy-making officials—department and division heads, commissioners, and personal assistants to these top people—does not fall within this definition of patronage. A chief executive must be free to surround himself with officials sensitive to his methods, and in agreement with his programs, but he will risk a dangerous blunder if he does not make certain that the men selected also have the character, ability and knowledge for the work. He chooses these men from colleges, from private enterprise, from other governments, and sometimes from persons who may be of the opposition. The fact that these top people generally are members of his political faith should not cause these appointments to be classed as patronage or spoils. Such appointments are an essential part of the democratic process; they bring into posts where policies are formulated men who share the philosophy of the party voted into office or of the chief executive in the case of non-partisan elections.[10] And they share the public accountability which is also integral to the democratic process. A competent mayor uses this freedom to build a strong working team, the members of which share the political views which won for him the election at the polls.

The rising education and political standards of the public and the professionalization of important segments of the public service (such as social work, health, planning, urban renewal, city management) together tend to limit the scope of spoils politics. These trends have been accompanied by occupational standards defined by, to some extent enforced by, and persistently policed by national professional associations and their local groups. The continued acceptance of the city manager system, for example, has fostered a new and growing profession of appointive chief executives separated from partisan politics and committed to seek professional colleagues.

The second false assumption held by many personnel administrators is that there is an ample supply of talent,

[10] In Denver, for example, the Charter allows the mayor to make 50 administrative appointments, and allows him some latitude in creating the list of positions to be made exempt from the competitive service.

and governments need only select the best from a wealth of qualified applicants. This was largely true during the depression. But for more than two decades there has been a shortage of capable people in many of the specialties most needed by local government.

There is little evidence, however, that local governments are revising their concepts of personnel administration. To the contrary, a special study conducted for the Commission concluded that there is no widespread agreement about what changes are needed for the future.[11] There are, unhappily, few signs of development of a positive philosophy of personnel administration in urban governments.

3. *The selection, hiring, promotion and disciplining of personnel, a fundamental element of management in any enterprise, is in too many urban governments artificially separated from and independent of the chief executive.* A basic and integral part of the task of management, in private and public enterprise alike, involves the selection, hiring, promotion and discipline of personnel. The case for managerial authority should not have to be recounted at length. Clarence Ridley, who for 27 years observed and studied local government as executive director of the International City Managers' Association, stated it tersely: "It seems quite clear that no administrator can be held strictly accountable for administrative results unless he retains final authority over personnel." [12]

[11] Griffenhagen-Kroeger, Inc., "Personnel Concepts and Practices for Modern Urban Government," prepared for the Commission.

[12] Clarence Ridley, "The Personnel Functions in Municipal Management," *Public Personnel Review,* July, 1945, p. 165.

In this discussion, by "independent commission" is meant an agency of the local government with authority that limits the freedom of the chief executive to hire, develop, discipline and dismiss the personnel which he directs and supervises.

The degrees of independence from the executive vary from state to state, and from government to government, making impossible any accurate estimate of the number of independent civil service commissions in local governments. Some are created by statute, and are "independent" by virtue of the method by which they were created. Other bodies are called independent because they are appointed by agencies other than the chief executive; others because their terms are long, they cannot be removed from office, or in some other way are insulated from the executive. Some simply become independent in their manner of operation.

One clue to the extent of these conditions can be found in the distribution of responsibility for actual personnel functions. Approximately 70 per cent of cities over 100,000 population and about 60 per cent of cities over 50,000 have vested final decision on dismissal and disciplinary appeals in an independent appeals body.[13] In most of these cities, a sizable segment of the personnel function—in rule making, examinations, certification for appointment, and promotions—is vested in a commission, not directly in the chief executive.

[13] *Municipal Year Book,* 1961, p. 164.

Handicaps Are Imposed on Administrators

Any significant separation of personnel functions and responsibilities obviously imposes serious handicaps on the chief administrator and his department heads. Local executives have made this abundantly clear to the Commission's staff. The chief executive of a large urban county stated bluntly that the traditional civil service system "breaks the chain of command" and tends to "line up the employees with the Civil Service Commission against the public official and thereby destroys the capacity of the administrator to function."

"This city," one official in a large industrial city added, "is being run *for* Civil Service."

Management often finds itself unable to determine its own manpower requirements, to rotate personnel as part of their development, or to promote primarily on the basis of ability.

In a large number of units in which staff interviews were conducted, officials emphasized their belief that unresponsive Civil Service Commissions and other independent personnel systems, when not in sympathy with management's needs, became the single most important obstacle to securing capable APT personnel.

Even more frustrating, according to many executives and officials, are the almost insuperable difficulties that confront the local governmental executive who would discipline or remove incompetents from their positions. Management's ability to direct and lead its staffs in getting the city's work done is thus further hampered. The independent Civil Service Commission, originally intended to be an impartial referee in employee-employer disputes, has, in many instances, a long history of bias on behalf of employees in disciplinary matters. For example, an official in a Massachusetts city commented: "The only way to remove a man is conviction for a felony or a misdemeanor involving moral turpitude. It is not easy."

> *It is almost impossible to fire a city employee. Almost all discharges which are appealed are overruled. In 11 years not one decision to dismiss by a manager has been sustained.*
>
> —MMC Staff field interview,
> Des Moines, Iowa, June, 1961

The lack of personnel authority often forces management into evasions of regulations.[14] These evasive maneuvers are done less for personal or political advantage than to advance the programs for which the officials are responsible. When officials recognize the need for able persons,

[14] Inflexible personnel systems sharpen the skills of operating officials in outwitting the rules. The Commission's investigations revealed more than a dozen common methods of evasion which are practiced by chief executives and department heads. Few are as extreme as that of one public health director who first places every resigning APT person in a "leave without pay" status until a qualified replacement becomes available. If none appears during this period, he abolishes the position, rather than be forced by regulations to accept a less-qualified applicant. If he can attract someone at a future date, he "reactivates" the job. Although not illegal, such maneuvers require a large expenditure of time and effort on the part of operating officials which might be better spent on program innovation.

they often try to get them even if normal recruiting and promotion methods do not work.

Civil Service Attitudes Preclude Reform from Within

Management's view that conventional civil service systems hamper good administration is given weight by the essentially negative approach of civil service administrators to the problems of management.

The Public Personnel Association reported that in most jurisdictions personnel directors held attitudes of distrust and trepidation toward their governments' chief administrators.[15] The possibility of spoils and patronage in some cities may justify this feeling, but such a feeling cannot promote or encourage meritorious performance, or help management achieve its personnel goals.

Personnel administrators prefer to invoke the specter of "spoils" as justification for separating the function from the executive. In a western city which relies on a "rule of one" in choosing persons for promotion—thus giving officials the choice of hiring this individual or no one—the personnel director said that to give officials a choice of three individuals would be a "retreat" and "an open invitation to the return of spoils."

Such attitudes are further illustrated from Municipal Manpower Commission staff studies. Civil service commis-

---

[15] The survey observed that cooperation and mutual confidence mark most units with effective recruitment. This relationship, the Public Personnel Association reported, appeared to be fundamental to successful personnel operations.

sion officials show an unwillingness to take aggressive measures to supply quality APT people. One large city's secretary for Civil Service states: "We strive for a high degree of mediocrity." In another city, a department head complained that the personnel director "is just a civil service policeman. He doesn't care at all about serving the operating departments." A mayor of a Connecticut city declared that the city's civil service commission "has generally made no attempt to attract superior people."

In summary, denying management authority over the personnel function constitutes a common problem for the local executive who has the responsibility to satisfy a demanding public. The creation of an independent Civil Service Commission does anything but help him in this matter. Indeed it often provides a handicapping stalemate. On the one hand, responsible administrators are frustrated by inflexible rules and regulations dictating who they may hire; who, when and how they shall promote; and whether, if at all, they may discipline or fire the incompetent or insubordinate. On the other hand, independent Civil Service officials, distrustful of the executives and seeking to prevent political favoritism and to protect the individual employee, devise additional limitations upon the executive's freedom to act.

4. *The compensation, career development and recruitment practices of most local governments are unequal to the task of getting and retaining the number and caliber of APT personnel required.*

Compensation

The salaries paid to administrative, professional and technical personnel are inadequate to enable local governments to compete for scarce talent. And the differentials in compensation between those in the employ of local governments and private firms in the same community tend to be greatest for public officials at the highest levels.

At a time when the federal government is seriously concerned with the compensation of its federal executives, there is scarcely any evidence that local governments have even considered the principle that public executives should receive salaries comparable to those of men and women doing like work in private positions.

Those few instances in which local officials command comparable salaries are almost invariably in special authorities and districts and are so unusual that they inspire a distorted public image of public service compensation. Compare the $31,000 salary of the general manager of the Omaha Public Power District with the $17,500 paid Omaha's Mayor. The manager of the Metropolitan Transit Authority of Boston receives $40,000; the Mayor of Boston is paid $20,000. Nearly always, however, professional salaries in local governments lag behind comparable employment elsewhere.

A Commission analysis of professional positions in 20 cities, 14 of them larger than 250,000 population, showed that in every category the average salary offered by the local governments was substantially below the national average paid to persons going into industry in 1961. For example, the beginning salary for professional accountants in the cities was $397 per month; the industry average was $462. In 1962 the average graduating senior going into private industry with a bachelor's degree in engineering will receive $560. In 1961, these 20 cities offered beginning engineers $437.

> *I do not believe MTA offers an exciting career opportunity for top college graduates. One of the reasons is that only a very few people receive the lucrative salaries that are usually reported in the press and elsewhere.*
>
> —MMC Staff field interview,
> Boston, Mass., June, 1961

For those professional occupations which do not have obvious counterparts in industry, the salary levels are still less. The average salary paid to a social case worker, who in most instances requires a minimum of a college degree in social work, was $336; for a bacteriologist, $365. Compare these with the $475 paid in 1961 to the average college graduate going into industry—regardless of his occupation.[16]

When top salaries remain relatively constant, higher entry level salaries telescope the top and bottom levels until there is less incentive to seek advancement. In Kentucky, for example, the state constitution limits the salary

[16] Industry averages from Frank A. Endicott, *Trends in Employment of College and University Graduates in Business and Industry, 1962,* Northwestern University, 1962, pp. 5-6.

of nearly all state and local officials to $7,200. Thus, an entry level planning assistant in Louisville's general purpose department can be paid about $4,600, but the director of the department receives only $2,600 more.

Salaries are a major source of dissatisfaction among more than one-third of all municipal executives. Nine out of ten believe that their salaries are not as high as comparable positions in private business, and 60 per cent believe that federal salaries would also be higher.[17]

Nationally, the compensation picture for administrative, professional and technical personnel, while not all black, shows local governments have failed to adjust their pay scales to enable them to compete effectively. The Commission notes that any financial sacrifice in local government service is borne most heavily by APT personnel inasmuch as office workers, laborers and skilled craftsmen usually have powerful political weapons to advance their wage demands with governments. For example, the study of 20 cities showed that a beginning electrician received an average salary of $458, while a beginning civil engineer was offered $437. The lowest step for a building inspector averaged $424, while that for a professional accountant was $397; for a bacteriologist, $365; for a social case worker, $336; and for a psychiatric social worker, $433. Lacking a lobby or a trade union, and sensitive to public criticism of their attempts to secure higher salaries, APT persons have become, in salary discussions, the forgotten people of local government.

[17] See Appendix 1, Profile of the Municipal Executive, Part IV.

Career Development

When talent is scarce, and new problems and responsibilities are mounting, progressive employers strive to develop the skills and capabilities of these men and women who make up their staffs. Yet this country's local governments are doing little to develop the persons who must bear vital responsibilities.

Training Is Weak. Less than one-third of local governments carry on any training for key administrative, professional, and technical people in their employ.[18] Most existing training is designed to improve the skills of office workers, police and firemen. Such "in-service training" does not focus on the key problem of developing APT personnel for the future needs of government.

> *We send some policemen to Northwestern University, and have several technical programs here in the Fire and Police Departments. For executives—we send some to conventions and they get some stuff there, but that's about all.*
>
> —MMC Staff field interview,
> Columbus, Ohio, June, 1961

This finding is based on the conclusions reached by the International City Managers' Association as a result of

[18] The International City Managers' Association found that the training for local governments' APT personnel is largely limited to specific functions of an employee's job. Only a minute number of those enrolled in APT training programs receive instruction dealing with the changing nature of local government, human relations, or decision making

their direct studies of 280 local governments. It is confirmed by a canvass of professional opinion conducted by the American Society for Public Administration.[19]

The failure of the local governments to invest in their own human resources is the more grievous because few other opportunities exist by which responsible and far-sighted local officials can develop the particular skills needed.

a) In only 12 states do the state governments conduct training for local officials in key positions. Of these, only New York provides an adequate state program of training opportunities for APT personnel in local government.

b) Fewer than half of the professional societies and associations, whose memberships include a significant part of APT employees, conduct training programs or courses in which APT personnel from local governments can participate.

c) In only a few cities do the local universities effectively assist in developing the local government's APT personnel. At least five universities, New York, Pennsylvania, Pittsburgh, Southern California and Wayne State, have programs that effectively contribute to the development of governmental personnel in their regions. But the need exists in each of the other 207 metropolitan areas where men and women are also striving to provide essential services for growing populations.

Career Opportunities Are Limited. Many local units are too small, or their departments too small, to provide

---

[19] ASPA reports most experts believe that efforts of local government to develop their personnel are not up to the existing need.

an adequate continuing challenge for trained men and women of high caliber and with strong motivation. Nearly four out of ten department and division heads in cities of less than 250,000 regard their opportunities for advancement as highly unsatisfactory. Consider, for example, the planning department of Lincoln, Nebraska. With a staff of only four, it is too small to provide career opportunities for the professionally trained men it includes. "Unless I leave," the planning director told the Commission's representatives, "a planner joining our staff has reached the top of his ladder within a short time after he joins us. Hence, I must look for a new planner to replace those who leave every two years." Or consider the future of the traffic engineer in Council Bluffs, Iowa: in his early twenties, he had reached the top of the ladder in this city and could go no higher unless he should become its city manager.

Mobility Is Limited. A greater share of this country's ablest young men and women could find satisfying careers in the service of local governments if they could climb from one local government to another, growing in experience and maturity, and assuming greater responsibilities. The prospect, however, of moving from a beginning position in a small city to a junior position in a larger one, and then to a smaller city in a senior position, and finally moving to a very large city at a senior level is drastically limited by prevailing practices of local governments.

As Chart 5 demonstrates, the average municipal executive has considerably less varied experience than business executives.

Yet, without mobility, the ablest and most highly motivated persons—those especially needed in expanding enterprises—may be denied the opportunity to develop to their potential. For professional persons in health, welfare, recreation and planning, mobility is somewhat greater than among public works, public safety, personnel, and finance specialists. Even professionals, however, often have difficulty moving from one local government to another, if restrictions are rigidly enforced.

There are many obstacles to effective mobility; among the most important are residence requirements, promotion from within, difficult-to-move retirement credits, and the lack of adequate information on job opportunities for APT personnel.

The requirement of legal residence as a prerequisite for appointment to—or in many cases application for—a position still exists in most of our urban governments. It is based on a mixture of local pride and a carry-over from earlier times of the charity concept of government employment—"we should use local money to take care of our own." One year is the most common requirement, but some two-year residence provisions are still being enforced.

Gradually this specification is being trimmed or eliminated; for shortage occupations and top APT personnel, waivers are becoming almost as common as strict enforcement. But to the extent these restrictions exist and are enforced they directly limit the mobility of APT personnel.

Promotion from within, widely acknowledged as of benefit to an enterprise, serves primarily as a means of preventing entry into a unit at middle or upper staff level. Personnel administrators confirm their reliance on promotion from within: in Dallas, San Francisco, St. Louis and other cities, examinations to fill vacancies are not open to outsiders, except as a last resort. "In 99 cases out of 100," stated a typical response to the Public Personnel Association survey, "our middle and top positions are filled by promotion."

> *I wouldn't start in San Francisco government now if I were starting over again in government, because of this combination: you start in at the bottom only, you have the rule of one throughout, you have examinations for every promotion, and this combination literally kills off any career possibilities.*
>
> —MMC Staff field interview, San Francisco, California July, 1961

Promotion from within does not, however, have corresponding success as an aid to career development. In governments of heavily populated areas, the many functions and departments should provide a very wide range of career lines, but promotional opportunities are often confined to personnel already in a given department. For example, in New York City, the civil service law and rules usually restrict appointments of most bureau chiefs to high-ranking members of the bureau who have taken a competitive promotion examination.[20] These traditional

[20] Wallace S. Sayre and Herbert Kaufman, *Governing New York City* (New York: Russell Sage Foundation, 1960), p. 233.

methods of competition are jealously guarded to give an advantage to the insiders.

Retirement systems in local governments have spread rapidly, making this aspect of public employment, in many areas, more competitive with private employment. At the same time, they have become an obstacle to easy movement of APT personnel.

In a handful of states, retirement credits can be moved easily between local and state employment, and immediate or early vesting of accumulated benefits makes it possible to move from a few systems without severe financial loss. In the vast majority of states and urban governments, however, retirement credits have turned into an anchor, and operate as a real deterrent to the easy interchange of middle and top level APT personnel.

The APT person looking for an opportunity to advance in his career faces an additional obstacle in the lack of information about job opportunities in local governments. It is difficult to find out about higher level vacancies which are open to outsiders. Local units do not aggressively distribute news about openings. A few professional organizations provide minimal clearinghouse functions, but these are not enough to serve the career needs of most local APT employees.[21]

[21] A review of the personnel recruitment and placement activities of 39 professional organizations indicates the existence of only a small number of personnel referral systems. Eight of the 39 organizations maintain extensive listings of job opportunities within their fields, and in some cases placement service on the pattern of a commercial agency, though on a non-profit basis. Twenty-four of the associations provide at least a minimal listing of job opportunities and/or applicant availability in their regular publications. These activities, however, are hampered by the fact

CHART 5

Municipal Executives Are Less Mobile than Business Executives

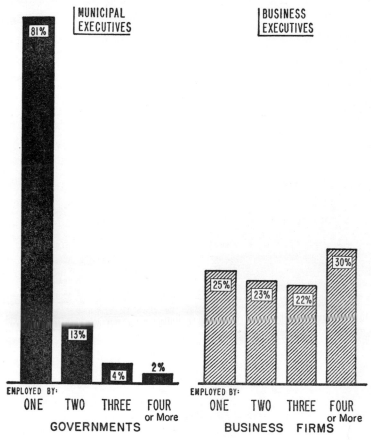

Source: Warner and Abegglen "Occupational Mobility in American Business and Industry", and Municipal Manpower Commission.

State leagues of municipalities do less. Some 18 league publications, none of which has national distribution, list a grand total of about 100 vacancies per issue. Of the 33 leagues replying to a Public Administration Service questionnaire, only California maintained an extensive file of positions and applicants. The actions by others in providing information was notably less.

Recruitment. The human resources of any enterprise must be continually replenished. Young people must be brought in at the bottom. APT personnel in various areas must be supplied to meet particular needs, and must be brought into the system when and where needed.

In relation to these obvious needs, local governments are notably weak in advancing manpower planning, application of recruiting techniques and provisions of funds—three of the basic elements of the recruitment process.

> *The principal reason for the manpower shortage in our department is that the Civil Service Commission has not been able to recruit. They have not had a positive recruitment program and there has been no response to ads and very little response to college recruiting.*
>
> —MMC Staff field interview, Detroit, Mich., June, 1961

Only three out of 60 units investigated by the staff attempt advance planning of manpower needs, despite the

that only two of the organizations provide any screening or testing of applicants, and only five seem to have adequate means of keeping their files current. The survey was conducted by Public Administration Service for the Commission.

fact that "modern organizations plan for filling managerial posts five, ten, or even twenty years ahead," according to O. Glenn Stahl.[22]

Chart 6 indicates the poor effectiveness of local government recruiting at the campus level, where intensive competition exists, according to college placement offices. This is compounded by local governments' failure to do regular recruiting on college campuses.[23] Even in larger governments, visits to campuses are sporadic; examinations are seldom keyed to the school year; firm job offers are slow in coming.

This passive approach does not take into account the many opportunities that face today's graduates. In 1961, less than one month after the end of the school year, about 90 per cent of engineering graduates were already committed to job, military service, or postgraduate studies. Another 5 per cent were weighing job offers. Most business and liberal arts graduates were also decided on their future plans, with only a small proportion uncommitted.[24]

Funds to permit flexibility in recruiting are lacking, and payment for interview and moving expenses is rare, although many companies consider such expenses as vital to a good recruitment effort.

In a large number of cities, there is rigid insistence upon hiring only residents. This has cut off the unit from the

[22] O. Glenn Stahl, Public Personnel Administration (New York: Harper and Brothers, 1956), p. 369.

[23] Among the 60 units visited by the staff, two units have continuous college recruiting programs; six occasionally recruited on campus for engineers and other critical specialists. The rest did none.

[24] Engineering Manpower Commission, Engineers Joint Council, The 1961 Engineering Graduate Placement Survey (New York, 1961), p. 17.

bulk of possible replacements when key positions are vacated. In other cities, the commitment to promotion from within, if at all possible, has also forestalled major recruitment efforts at the middle level. The net result is the weakening of input both at the entry level and also in the middle echelon ranges, where experience and maturity are particularly important.

5. *The quality of APT personnel in local governments today, by and large, is inadequate to cope with present and especially emerging metropolitan problems.* A working en-

CHART 6

Local Government Recruiting Suffers by Comparison

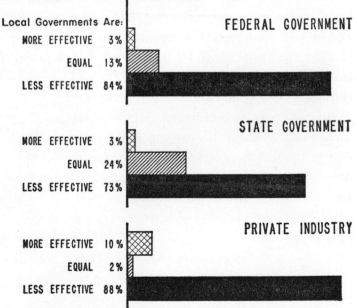

Local Governments Are:

FEDERAL GOVERNMENT

MORE EFFECTIVE	3%
EQUAL	13%
LESS EFFECTIVE	84%

STATE GOVERNMENT

MORE EFFECTIVE	3%
EQUAL	24%
LESS EFFECTIVE	73%

PRIVATE INDUSTRY

MORE EFFECTIVE	10%
EQUAL	2%
LESS EFFECTIVE	88%

Source: Municipal Manpower Commission

vironment that does not attract able men and women and
personnel systems that restrict executives in their personnel
powers largely account for today's picture of mediocrity
in local government.

There are able, competent and dedicated men and
women in key positions in local governments—but not
nearly enough. The Commission's investigations revealed
some outstanding individuals, and a few governments with
a high caliber of manpower throughout its APT positions.

In a large number of cities a thin layer of top level career
men makes possible the meeting of some of today's problems. Five years ago, the Editors of *Fortune* wrote what the
Commission has more recently observed: "To many a big-
city government, hard pressed to find money to maintain
essential services, much less to provide new ones, the pres-
ence of a band of top professionals at City Hall has probably meant the difference between success and failure in
operating the big service machine." [25]

In other local governments the heads of a few departments, usually those carrying on the more recently organized functions of government such as planning, urban renewal and housing, display skill, creativity and enterprise.
In a few cities, top level performance in these functions has
helped improve the level of performance in other city departments. But a candid evaluation of the executives of this
country's local governments, viewed as a body, reveals dis-
couraging evidences of the capabilities of this total group.

[25] Seymour Freedgood, "New Strength in City Hall," *The Exploding
Metropolis* (New York, Doubleday, 1957), p. 79.

> *There are many competent 30–45 year-old men right now, many with World War II service and maybe a touch of governmental experience, who could be brought into the local government about this time to fill the middle gap, were it not for their lack of professional experience and its relationship to the specific requirements of rigid Civil Service Systems.*
>
> –MMC Staff field interview, San Francisco, California August, 1961

Below the executive level, quality is even more suspect. Civic leaders and public officials repeatedly stated that the persons in traditional functions, such as public works, public safety, libraries, sanitation, were simply not well enough prepared, either as specialists or as administrators, to assume key positions in their governments. Yet the attrition above them and the promotion policies that prevail will place them in positions where decisions for the future must be made.

a. *In a significant number of instances, local governments are living on the "fat" of the manpower they were able to recruit during the depression Thirties.* Almost half of today's urban executives entered the service of their government prior to 1940 when the competition of private business for able people was not as great.[26]

In the 1930's, although local governments added relatively few persons to their total employment, selection was

[26] For details, see Appendix 1, Profile of the Municipal Executive.

rigorous, with several thousand persons often competing on a single examination in larger cities. For many of the entrants during these years, local government was not the first choice, but business offered few opportunities for employment.

In recent years, particularly since 1945, local governments have suffered a continuing erosion of their human resources. The ability of competing employers to offer more satisfying opportunities and greater compensation and the rigidity of many Civil Service systems, as discussed previously, have caused many able men and women to leave their positions in local government.

b. *The retirement of a large proportion of all department and division heads in the next decade must be expected.* Thirty-eight per cent of municipal department heads and 31 per cent of division heads are within ten years of age sixty-five. As Chart 7 shows, superannuation is not uncommon among department heads.

In some governments, the frequency of over-sixty-five executives is a serious problem. At the time staff interviews were held in a midwestern city of 125,000, the city treasurer was past sixty-five, his deputy was sixty-four, and two other ranking members of the division were sixty-five and seventy-six. The public works director was past seventy, and the tax commissioner was sixty. In an Ohio city, a top official said that a majority of his 13 division heads will retire in the near future. Department chiefs in their eighties continue to bear significant responsibilities in other large cities.

The problems posed by the age factor are scarcely being met by manpower planning on the part of local governments. As Chart 7 also indicates, only one in 20 cities plans its personnel needs at least one year in advance.

In the opinion of local officials and civic observers in

CHART 7

Municipal Executives Close to Retirement

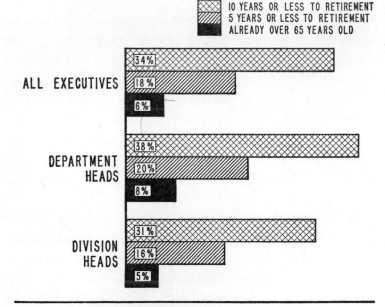

10 YEARS OR LESS TO RETIREMENT
5 YEARS OR LESS TO RETIREMENT
ALREADY OVER 65 YEARS OLD

ALL EXECUTIVES
34%
18%
6%

DEPARTMENT HEADS
38%
20%
8%

DIVISION HEADS
31%
16%
5%

FEW CITIES DO COMPREHENSIVE MANPOWER PLANNING

WITH PLANS   NO MANPOWER PLANS
5%   95%

Source: Municipal Manpower Commission

communities from coast-to-coast, there are too few likely successors within the systems to match the abilities of to-day's aging officials.

c. *In the opinion of their peers many APT people in local governments are poorly prepared for their positions.* This is the summation of the judgments of professional public administrators in 16 centers throughout the country. These judgments are in part supported (and perhaps partially explained) by data as to the educational training of local governmental officials.

Only one in five public safety directors and less than half of all finance directors graduated from college. Only two of ten finance directors hold degrees in business administration, accounting or economics. In addition, in cities under 250,000, slightly more than one of three division heads is a college graduate.[27]

We do get a few good recruits but most of them won't stay long. Many of our young men are good technicians, but they do not have a broad enough background to move up the ladder and eventually become top administrators.

–MMC Staff field interview,
Westchester County, New York
June, 1961

---

d. *The local governments have not attracted, at the entry level, a fair share of the ablest young people equipped with intelligence and training to rise to APT positions.* Recruit-

[27] See Appendix 1, Profile of the Municipal Executive.

ment officers of the local governments repeatedly testified that they cannot compete for the ablest graduates of the colleges, engineering schools and universities. "We get such men as we can from the third and fourth quartiles of the graduating classes" was the pessimistic observation of one city manager. A public works director in another city similarly observed that his department was drawing "from the bottom one-third of the engineering classes, and these are not from the top schools."

Underlying this problem of lack of quality at entry level are two related conditions: the appeal of the local government as an employer to young people is feeble in comparison with that of other employers; few university programs prepare students, especially in professional or technical fields, for service in urban local government, and these few programs attract a small share of the abler students.

In summary, such evidences as there are of the quality of today's APT personnel in local governments—evidences of their age, training, and experience; observation of their vitality and performance; and the judgment of their peers in the public service—raise substantial doubts as to whether this body of men and women is equal to the changing role of local governments and the new, large and challenging responsibilities that are to be thrust upon them. More serious is the companion conclusion that few of today's civic, political, and administrative leaders are alert to this inadequacy and its implications in the face of tomorrow's manpower needs.

4

Recommendations:
An Agenda for Metropolis

A direct, massive effort must be launched to attract and hold more and better-equipped APT persons in local governments. But this critical problem cannot be solved apart from two other vital problems confronting our metropolises. If we are to improve manpower, there must also be:

1. Improved governmental structure, i.e., better organization to link the governments of areas, already inextricably related by geographical, economic, and social ties, into an effective working team. Conversely, the Commission believes that such improvement will come sooner if the manpower problem is solved.

2. Earnest, broad-gauged, and persistent efforts on the part of civic leaders to define and work for objectives that advance the whole metropolitan community. In short,

89

there is an urgent need for imaginative, civic-minded leadership to set goals that will attract, provide incentive for, and establish clear directions for able APT personnel.

Action is essential. Only with better qualified manpower in public office, improved governmental institutions, and energetic, far-sighted leaders of community groups, can the citizens of metropolitan areas look forward to better living conditions and greater satisfaction in community activities.

THE LONG-RANGE PROSPECT UNCERTAIN

For the long-range future, the rapidly mounting population in metropolitan areas threatens to pose problems of such magnitude that more and better public personnel, better governmental structure, and imaginative and energetic community leaders may be unable to overcome them.

Both the increasing rate of population growth and the continuing movement from rural to urban areas will apparently accentuate this metropolitan problem of American life. For instance, the best available statistics indicate the possibility of a metropolitan area population of 295,-000,000 in the year 2000. This is more than double the present metropolitan population. If the rate of growth is not slowed, all our present urban and suburban facilities— homes, streets, schools, stores and shopping centers—must be duplicated in little more than one generation. We and our children must find the tremendous capital required, clear sufficient land, and more than double all existing metropolitan areas before the end of this century.

We suggest no solution to the population problem as such, but we are convinced that some solution must be found. Our growing urban population and its continually increasing drain on the resources of local governments poses so many problems of such magnitude and consequence to the American people as to call urgently for further intensive study and for early national and local decisions.

THE SHORT-RANGE PROSPECTS

In advance of the time when such decisions are arrived at through the democratic process, the working environment of urban local governments needs to be improved in four ways:

1. Leaders must join forces to define metropolitan objectives.

2. Every metropolitan community should formulate a total metropolitan plan.

3. Metropolitan areas must develop improved agencies and institutions for permanent and effective governmental teamwork and action.

4. A partnership of local, state and federal governments should encourage comprehensive metropolitan planning and action.

ACTIONS NEEDED TO
RESHAPE THE METROPOLITAN ENVIRONMENT

The challenge of local public service will not be attractive without actions by governmental units and by civic and political leaders.

Local Governments Should:

• Cooperate with each other in metropolitan areas to devise effective arrangements capable of resolving metropolitan-wide problems while preserving neighborhoods and communities.

• Seek necessary legislative and administrative support from state and federal governments to permit greater ability to meet problems at the local level.

State Governments Should:

• Revise constitutions and laws to give local governments more opportunity to provide and finance essential public services.

• Encourage new governmental arrangements in metropolitan areas for the effective handling of area-wide problems.

The Federal Government Should:

• Make a strenuous effort to coordinate all federal programs which have an impact on the development of metropolitan areas.

• Continue to stimulate metropolitan planning and follow-through by extending the "workable program" concept to grants-in-aid aimed at communities.

All Governments Should:

• Cooperate with the various levels of government to improve coordination of programs and policies which have an impact on the planning and development of metropolitan areas.

Civic and Political Leadership Should:

• Organize on a metropolitan-area-wide basis, formally or informally.

• Study, define, and promote metropolitan community objectives.

• Propose actions which would achieve these objectives.

RESHAPING THE ENVIRONMENT

1. *Civic, business and governmental leadership must join forces to define metropolitan community objectives.* The community leaders of each metropolitan area must accept responsibility for leadership on metropolitan problems, as well as on the problems of their own local communities. If they do not foresee the future needs of the whole metropolitan community, plan to meet them, and arouse the interest of citizens in each locality in carrying out such plans, they will not provide the needed stimulus for local governments.

Area leadership must unite to study metropolitan problems, to encourage metropolitan planning, and to help move toward governmental institutions having the power to formulate plans and translate them into reality.

There exists in every metropolitan area leadership capable of creating effective arrangements; each area must choose the approach suited to its needs. The basic unit may be a small committee of key economic, social and political leaders representative of the metropolitan area. Or it may be a much larger council including representatives from many organizations, governmental units and neighborhoods.

Fortunately, there are useful precedents for those who wish to move ahead. A growing number of formal and informal organizations are active in metropolitan areas. Most sponsor studies and research, but several have gone further by reaching agreement on proposals for action and then by taking the necessary steps to accomplish them.

Some of these groups are composed largely of business-men and professionals. They range from the informal gathering, such as Los Angeles' Town Hall, to the highly structured organization, such as Pittsburgh's Allegheny Conference, the Bay Area Council in the San Francisco area, and the Greater Philadelphia Movement.

Other organizations primarily deal with metropolitan problems and objectives. For 35 years, the New York Regional Plan Association has performed this important service; similar bodies are following its example. Some were created specifically to do research in metropolitan problems: Cleveland's Metro, Philadelphia's Penjerdel—a tri-state project—and the Washington Center for Metropolitan Studies—sponsored by seven local universities, officials, and business and civic groups.

These organizations are widely varied. Whatever the policy-making device, however, their experience indicates one essential feature if continuing progress is to be made. There must be financial support for a professional staff, research contracts, and a wide range of educational and promotional programs. Money ought to be supplied by those whose future welfare is most at stake—local business enterprises and local foundations.

2. *Every metropolitan community should formulate a total metropolitan plan—physical, social and fiscal.* The health of a community depends upon a host of diversified actions. In the metropolis, each of these activities relates

to and reacts upon other activities. The kind of development within the metropolitan area depends upon the quality of each of these activities and on how well each relates to the goals and objectives of the entire metropolitan community.

There must, therefore, be effective metropolitan planning. To harmonize each of these activities and the conflicting community interests within each metropolitan area there must be agreement on broad community objectives. Out of the planning process must come program priorities, so that objectives will not only be stated but carried out. As part of the planning process therefore there must be not only objectives but agreement on the laws, the organizational arrangements, the fiscal plans and the administrative procedures necessary to achieve such objectives.

By definition metropolitan planning is not limited to governmental action. Governmental activities and facilities merely form the framework within which development and redevelopment take place; the planning process must embrace and relate to the many activities of private enterprise, educational agencies, professions and other non-governmental organizations concerned with the metropolitan society.

To some extent, this is already taking place. But, although there are a number of public, and private, metropolitan planning agencies, the efforts of most such agencies have not yet gone beyond the early, developing stage. These agencies are concerned with the gathering of the information on which planning objectives can be based.

These agencies are, however, making progress; they are accumulating experience, gradually building an art or science of planning, and striving for worthy objectives.

For the most part, current planning programs are directed at specific functions and activities. As these planning efforts and the skills of planners are developed they should help the citizens they serve define the strengths and weaknesses of the whole metropolitan economy, and foresee the demands for facilities (e.g., streets, freeways, libraries, junior colleges, and airports) and for services (e.g., radiation control, elimination of water pollution) that a future population will place on the metropolitan area.

To achieve the results of metropolitan planning may depend on new forms of government with metropolitan-wide authority. But the planning process cannot be deferred until these forms exist. Every metropolitan area should organize now to underwrite a metropolitan planning agency and to carry out planning objectives.

3. *In the metropolitan areas, we must develop improved agencies and institutions for permanent and effective governmental teamwork and action.* That metropolitan area which is not actively working to create new governmental arrangements to cope with metropolitan-wide problems is not responding to the challenge of the 1960's. What is needed is an organizational structure that facilitates consideration of metropolitan-wide problems, that preserves the identity and strengths of local neighborhoods, and makes for effective action in providing more and better governmental services. This Commission is concerned with

manpower; it does not presume to propose the form of government that is required if more able men and women are to be attracted and retained in the employ of local governments.

Already, several metropolitan areas have devised arrangements that simultaneously cope with metropolitan problems and preserve the social values of each local neighborhood and community ways adopted to their own peculiar needs. City-county consolidation has worked well in Baton Rouge. In Los Angeles, the county performs one or more services on a contractual basis for almost every incorporated unit within the county.

Metropolitan government is another widely-discussed approach to resolving structural obsolescence. The types and powers of metropolitan governments range from a single centralized body empowered to conduct all the activities of government for the entire area, to a federated structure in which the central government assumes certain functions but the towns and other units retain others— much as the 50 states retain many powers under the U.S. Constitution.

Metropolitan Dade County is a ground-breaking experiment in metropolitan government. In neighboring Canada, metropolitan Toronto has built a solid record of achievement. Both the Dade County and the Toronto approaches preserve towns and cities. In fact, the Dade County charter retains a simple process of incorporation and the creation of new municipalities is no more difficult than before adoption of the metropolitan form.

Special districts and authorities have also demonstrated their effectiveness in dealing with separate metropolitan problems, such as sewage, water or parks. In the New York and other large metropolitan areas, these units of government have accomplished much.

Regional councils provide another precedent for further action. These councils, composed of elected officials from all or most of the governmental units in a metropolitan area, are helpful in defining common problems and in undertaking cooperative action in some fields.

Through the New York Metropolitan Regional Council, for example, top elected officials of 21 counties and 16 cities are working together for the future of this huge metropolis. Similarly the Washington Metropolitan Regional Conference has made progress in bringing together local officials of the District of Columbia and of the suburban governments, and the Congressmen who represent the Maryland and Virginia portions of this interstate region. At least four other regional councils have been formed elsewhere.[1]

New forms of government may or may not result from these efforts. But these arrangements promise more effective intergovernmental cooperation and better understanding of the need for both metropolitan planning and metropolitan-wide action.

4. *The state and federal governments, in a three-way partnership with urban local governments, should encourage comprehensive metropolitan planning and action.* The

[1] The San Francisco, Detroit, Salem (Oregon) and Wichita (Kansas) areas have established forms of official cooperation.

solution of metropolitan problems is not the province of local governments alone. The interests of federal and state governments are also involved. In such governmental functions as highways and social welfare, for example, policies, programs, and services already reflect federal, state, and local decisions.

In the future, there must be greater recognition and acknowledgement that all levels of governments have a responsibility for resolving metropolitan problems. They must perfect a working partnership which employs the abilities and authority of each, if the federal system is to continue to be effective.

States

Conditions in the 50 states vary, but one conclusion is clear. Every state must re-examine the role of local government in metropolitan areas and arrive at a state-local policy which will permit constructive governmental action in metropolitan areas.

State action may take the form of strengthening the authority of existing cities and counties to undertake those additional services which citizens demand, to recruit and pay personnel in accordance with the needs of local government, and to exercise more realistic planning controls over new urban development.

It may take the form of revising governmental structure and creating new metropolitan-wide governments with limited or general responsibility in the framework of new concepts of home rule.

It may take the form of state action to raise the level of local governmental performance, in the same way that federal requirements for a "workable program" have stimulated planning in urban areas throughout the country.

It may take the form of state support for either an administrative agency or a continuing research program directed toward year-to-year evaluation of local action to meet urban problems. There is a major need for machinery at the state level which can analyze the financial capacity of local governments, propose statutory modifications to permit better performance by local government, encourage changes in governmental structure needed for more efficient administration, and review productive experiments in other states so that new ideas will quickly be put to use.

Let us re-emphasize that no single pattern of government will be applicable in all states. But fresh ideas are available, and the need is for exploration and experimentation. Several states are seriously studying their responsibility to metropolitan areas. New York has established an Office of Local Government to pursue research and encourage coordination of state-local action. Minnesota is experimenting with a state agency to take on the thorny problem of local governmental boundaries. North Carolina has formulated a strong policy for urban areas and has granted cities broad annexation and extra-territorial planning powers, granted counties land use controls, and made construction of state highways inside municipalities dependent on joint adoption by the state and the municipality of a major thoroughfare plan.

As a basis for evaluating what is needed and what is being done, the Advisory Commission on Intergovernmental Relations is pursuing a constructive program and furnishing many valuable suggestions.[2]

In the 24 interstate metropolitan areas which overlap state boundaries, the states must cooperate to solve a myriad of problems, the resolution of which is made peculiarly difficult by the essentiality of observing the sovereign rights of the states involved. There should be much greater reliance on the interstate compact—a good example is the Port of New York Authority—to cope with problems of water supply, transportation, planning and sewage treatment. To be most effective, such compacts ought to permit the handling of several urban governmental functions.

Federal

The impact of federal activities on metropolitan areas requires better coordination of its programs. The federal government must establish some organizational machinery for this purpose.

What machinery will best meet this need is vigorously contested by those who propose establishment of a department of urban affairs, and those who would establish a coordinating unit within the Executive Office of the President. This Commission has not equipped itself to resolve this question. But it is patent that the federal government

[2] Especially useful on the Advisory Commission's Report A-5, "Governmental Structure, Organization and Planning in Metropolitan Areas," July 1961; and an account of accomplishments and plans in the "Third Annual Report," January 31, 1962.

either must take immediate steps in this direction or must accept responsibility for accentuating the metropolitan problem even while it strives to resolve segments of the whole problem.

The federal government's partnership role should also involve increased incentive for effective state and local action on metropolitan problems. Several actions point the way; (1) federal grants are available now for metropolitan planning, and (2) local governments must have a Program of Community Improvement (workable program) [3] and must be making progress toward carrying out that program in order to receive grants for urban renewal and community facilities. Similarly, any area receiving federal aid for mass transportation must have a program for the development of a comprehensive and coordinated mass transportation system. In the new open space program, grants are dependent upon the existence of an area-wide plan.[4]

The federal government can give substantial impetus to local efforts by applying such requirements to other programs of federal assistance, and by specifying high procedural standards for the conduct of these activities at the local level. In particular, federal assistance should be con-

[3] The Housing Act of 1954 authorizes grants for "planning work in metropolitan and regional areas to official state, metropolitan or regional planning agencies empowered under state or local laws to perform such planning." (Sec. 701 [a-2].)

[4] The Housing Act of 1961 provides, "No contract for a grant may be made unless the Administrator finds that (1) the proposed use of land for permanent open space is important to the execution of a comprehensive plan for the urban area, and (2) a program of comprehensive planning is being actively carried on for the area." (Sec. 703.)

ditioned on plans covering the whole metropolitan area, rather than only single units of government. The purpose of federal grants should be to help communities do the things they want to do, but to do them better and on an adequate scale. The basic initiative must remain with the local community leaders—both civic and governmental.

Metropolitan problems are of such magnitude as to be of national significance. If local leadership fails to recognize and meet these needs, the national interest will require inevitably greater federal intervention and direction, rather than impetus and advice.

As a further aid to the solution of problems which plague interstate metropolitan areas, Congress should consider the enactment of legislation which would give advance approval to certain types of interstate compacts, with particular emphasis upon compacts which would encourage greater coordination of activities such as water supply, transportation, planning and sewage treatment.

ACTIONS NEEDED TO ACHIEVE
MANAGEMENT, MERIT, AND MANPOWER GOALS

The attainment of goals discussed in this chapter depends largely on actions by governments, voluntary organizations, and individuals. Some of the most important steps are listed here.

Local Governments Should:

• Enact an ordinance which endorses merit principles and places full responsibility for carrying out these principles in the chief executive.

• Develop satisfying career opportunities for APT personnel by rapid promotion of qualified employees and by removal of barriers which keep out experienced persons for middle-rank positions.

• Recruit vigorously both at college level and among experienced public officials, on a nation-wide, continuing basis where necessary.

• Make salaries for APT positions competitive.

• Provide adequate administrative and financial support to ensure modern personnel administration.

• Establish comprehensive post-entry training programs to prepare APT personnel for higher, broader responsibilities.

• Undertake much greater cooperation with other governments to improve any or all of these conditions, particularly in training, recruitment, and career development.

State Governments Should:

• Abolish any legal barriers which prevent local governments from fixing responsibility for personnel management in the chief executive.

• Establish a state-wide retirement system based on transferability of credits so that an employee may move from one public employer to another.

• Encourage national efforts toward a nation-wide retirement system for all public employees.

The Federal Government Should:

• Make certain that local governments which receive grants-in-aid are adequately staffed with APT personnel who have responsibility for carrying out programs.

• Provide fellowships, perhaps on a matching-dollar basis, for the career education of APT personnel in urban service.

• Cooperate with states to establish fully transferable retirement credits between both retirement systems, thus encouraging greater mobility of APT personnel.

Professional Associations Should:

• Reflect greater awareness of the impact of urbanization on professional skills, qualifications, and standards.

• Establish national rosters for their professions to encourage more effective recruitment, greater mobility, and better use of professionals in the public service.

• Support regional and national clearinghouses for greater exchange of information on the identity, qualifications, and availability of APT personnel.

Universities Should:

• Review and revise graduate and undergraduate programs to emphasize the significance of metropolitanization in American society.

• Emphasize early professional education for APT careers in public service.

• Seek stronger financial support for fellowships in urban curricula.

• Make available career training programs in every major urban center by means of cooperation between state universities and colleges and university branches in metropolitan areas.

Civic and Political Leadership Should:

• Insist on quality among APT personnel in the local government.

• Give aggressive, mature support to movements to establish management-oriented merit systems.

• Exert influence wherever possible to make manpower a significant political issue.

MANAGEMENT, MERIT, AND MANPOWER

There is an immediate need for improving the quality of governmental manpower. Furthermore, changes in personnel management can be made more quickly and easily than changes in the environment, and more capable people in key jobs will pay high dividends in the quality of these critical decisions.

Recommendations

Specifically, we recommend prompt and substantial improvements along five lines.

1. *The chief executive should be given clear-cut authority for personnel administration.* The executive who manages a growing, changing urban government must have authority over the personnel on whom he depends to get his work done. Urban mayors, city managers, division heads and others of like rank in urban counties must have greater authority to hire, to promote, to discipline and to fire. These integral elements of management should not be subject to control by an independent commission or by political influences.

Government, like business, cannot afford the uncertain performance of weak management. It is particularly important that control of the key administrative, professional and technical personnel be vested in the executive. He should be permitted to select his department heads and other key subordinates with as few limits as possible in terms of seniority, the definition of qualifications acquired, the classification of those positions, establishment and carrying out of promotion and transfer and the handling of appeals.

Where patronage and spoils still prevail, the chief executive must be protected against those who would build their own political organization without regard for the effectiveness of local government. In addition, means should be devised to safeguard personnel from arbitrary or discriminatory treatment, but without depriving the chief executive the essential authority to hire, promote, discipline and dismiss personnel.

Obviously, some high policy-making positions in any government must be filled by the appointment of capable individuals sharing the political views and interests of elected officials and legislators. Such appointments are essential to assure that the governmental machinery is responsive to the will of the electorate expressed in elections.[5] Local ordinances should be enacted to ensure that the selection and promotion of men and women in all career positions are carried out on the basis of merit. Any regulations, however, must allow the chief executive and his department head wide latitude. It is up to them to display the courage and integrity required to combat the spoilsman.

[5] Griffenhagen-Kroeger, Inc., after discussing the place of "politics" in the appointment of local officials, suggested "the concept that all political considerations are evil *per se*, be dropped; for as long as it remains a part of our thinking it unduly conditions other concepts and practices. It gives them a protective, negative coloration which stands in the way of making personnel administration an effective part of management."

2. *The independent civil service commission, where it exists, should be abolished or limited to an advisory function.* The *independent* civil service commission, a foundation-stone of the movement for better government for three-quarters of a century, has outlived its usefulness as an instrument of personnel management. Today, we must look to responsible mayors, city managers, and department heads to seek out and provide the experienced administrators, and the qualified professional and technical personnel that are required.

Hence, where an *independent* civil service commission now controls the recruitment, selection, compensation, training or promotion of personnel, it should be abolished or its authority and administrative functions should be limited to an advisory role.

The mature urban units of this country—those that have grown up politically and administratively—can operate perfectly well without an independent civil service commission. For those lacking maturity, or where some local situation of a compelling nature exists, a civil service commission can be used to perform important functions apart from personnel management.

First, such a commission, if staffed adequately, can serve a valuable purpose in hearing the appeals of employees against personal or political favoritism. Thus such a commission can aid the executive to withstand the pressures of veterans organizations, labor unions and business groups which might otherwise influence executives and council members.

Second, such a commission can build public acceptance and confidence by continually "auditing" or reviewing the government's personnel policies and practices in the interest of the public. An independent commission of this character is not solely a "watchdog," but could quickly become a strong ally to administrators in search of quality, and a powerful adversary of those who would misuse the personnel power.

3. *The appointment and advancement of public personnel should be based exclusively on merit principles.* The principle of "merit"—that men and women should be selected and promoted only on the basis of proved competence and accomplishment—must be observed in any enterprise faced with great changes and public responsibilities. In a profit-making enterprise, this principle is mandatory if management is to produce better goods and services at less cost and more profit. It is no less important in local government today, but it has been too often ignored. Modern personnel administration can build a merit system based on ability, performance on the job, and capacity for growth.

Professional personnel staffs are able to establish well-defined criteria of merit, and they can create procedural safeguards to insure fair employee treatment, without resorting to the artificial separation of the personnel function from the chief executive.

Illustrative is the Pasadena, California, executive merit system, which works smoothly without a civil service commission. A similar system operates in Winston-Salem and

Charlotte, North Carolina, and in a number of other cities.

The accompanying chart includes the essential elements on which management-centered merit systems should be based.

ELEMENTS OF MANAGEMENT-CENTERED MERIT SYSTEMS

1. A personnel ordinance or code which supports merit principles and clearly vests the responsibility for the personnel function in the chief executive.

2. A classification system for positions which states clearly the duties to be performed, the responsibilities to be assumed, and the education, experience and skill qualifications necessary.

3. Provision for determining these qualifications at entry and throughout each phase of career development, with promotions based on the periodic and planned evaluation of each individual occupying an APT position by his superiors (or his peers).

4. Appointment or promotion should not be based on seniority, upon the individual's status as a veteran or upon his or her residence within the municipality.

5. Provision for entry at higher levels through carefully devised programs to search for and secure the best APT talents, wherever they may be found.

6. Provision of effective staff assistance in personnel offices to analyze the performance and career requirements of APT personnel.

7. Provision for career development through careful placement, supervision, rotation, planned transfer, and post-entry educational opportunities for all APT personnel.

8. Appropriation of adequate funds to support the entire personnel function, from recruitment to retirement.

9. Dismissal and disciplinary procedures should be established and made known to all personnel. Responsibility for their application should be vested in department heads, subject to final review by the chief executive.

4. Personnel practices must be revitalized to provide rewarding careers. To meet the challenges of the 1960's, personnel administration in local governments must keep pace with the examples set by the federal government and many private businesses.

Men and women will grow if their day-to-day work provides a steadily widening range of professional experience, a visibly rising level of responsibility, broadening contacts with stimulating and capable individuals and increases in compensation that encourage the continual building of their administrative or professional ability. This, in sum, would constitute a challenging career.

a. Urban local governments must raise their present salary schedules to compete successfully for relatively scarce APT personnel. The total compensation of APT personnel must be comparable to that enjoyed by men and women of like skill, and bearing like responsibilities, in private employment and the more advanced public enterprises. This principle of comparability is, in the long run, economical in its application and is in the public interest. In a growing number of units it has been applied to the compensation of rank-and-file employees. It must also be applied to APT personnel if local governments are to get their share of the stream of young people who will be starting their careers in the next generation. They have a right to expect that urban service will permit them to live with a dignity appropriate to their position.

It may not be possible to provide salaries for officials at the department head and chief executive level identical to those obtained in many private enterprises. But no local government should have to depend on men and women who are satisfied with less compensation because they are second best, or because they can afford the luxury of public service.

To meet the competition of private business among graduating seniors in 1962, urban governments would have offered beginning engineers as much as $7,000; accountants up to $6,000; and the average June college graduate over $5,800.[6]

Many of our more progressive cities now base pay rates for personnel in clerical, stenographic, skilled and unskilled labor jobs on an annual pay survey which discloses the averages of wages paid by private employers. These studies seldom extend to the upper APT echelons and rarely are conducted by several governments in an area.[7]

The direct path to establishing an equitable and practi-

[6] Estimates based on survey of 215 "Well-known Business and Industrial Concerns." See: Frank S. Endicott, *Trends in Employment of College and University Graduates in Business and Industry* (Northwestern University, 1962), p. 6.

[7] An exception is the city of Denver, whose charter requires that all career employees be paid wages comparable to those employed in similar positions by local firms.

cal salary system for APT personnel is the cooperation of all local governments in a metropolitan area to study the compensation of workers in private enterprise doing work comparable to that of their own employees—from the bottom to the top of the public service.[8]

b. *Local governments must develop APT personnel for broader professional and executive duties.* In a "growth industry," there is a special need for updating the knowledge and developing the capabilities and understanding of APT people. This is essential if each local government is to meet ever more complex problems stemming from rapid growth. It is essential if the administrative, professionally or technically trained man is to keep abreast of advances in his field, and if each is to have a continuing opportunity to learn what others have already learned.

The chief executive and the department head should insure that APT personnel in each functional department are stimulated and aided to expand their own understanding and technical skills. This "continuing growth" will be furthered by application of the full range of training techniques, instructional methods, and materials. In addition, incentives for training should be established as an inducement to APT personnel.

[8] A breakthrough in the technique of comparability studies of top-level salaries can be found in studies made by the U.S. Civil Service Commission and the Bureau of Labor Statistics. Using a carefully prepared approach, the research team set bench marks for a combination of attributes and responsibilities of various top classes of federal employees, and for positions in private enterprises possessing similar characteristics. The resulting salary comparison formed the basis for the extensive reforms recommended by the President's Committee in February, 1962.

This makes essential further training in university programs, in institutes offered by professional associations, in in-service institutes or in other training programs. And it requires six steps on the part of individual governments:

1. Action by the chief executive to provide training which will help each of his colleagues develop the skills and understanding they need.

2. Employment, in the larger local governments at least, of competent training officers to work directly with the chief executive.

3. A policy of "continuing development" of employees, based on research into the needs of both the individual and the enterprise.

4. More comprehensive training to include preparation for higher positions and to aid specialists (e.g., social workers or engineers) to think and act like managers.

5. Use of the full range of training techniques and devices, as well as the best instructional methods and materials.

6. Provision of positive incentives to employees who do train, especially in using training as a criterion for promotion.

At the least, these actions are needed if local government is to attract and hold the caliber of men and women needed. To achieve them, many local governments will require the stimulus and support of federal and state government; that stimulus and support must include not only modest financial aid, but also the leadership and technical skill of men capable of planning and conducting training programs tailored to the needs of adjacent local governments.

Furnishing greater opportunities for personal growth for every person in an APT position must be recognized as a public responsibility for the public's benefit.

c. *Broader career opportunities must be provided for APT personnel.* A career system that relates advance to personal growth and to that alone is the only career system that will meet the needs of local governments. To develop the human resources essential to meet tomorrow's urban problems in an orderly fashion, and to attract the caliber of men and women required, the local governments must make available more attractive and satisfying careers than now exist. Local governments can broaden career opportunities substantially by taking four steps:

1. They must single out especially able men and women already within their employ.

2. They must examine and improve their utilization of these people's talents, ensuring that careers are not restricted to service within a single department or division, but that growth is fostered by a diversity of experience.

3. They must abandon excessive reliance on military service (veterans' preference), seniority, or political allegiance as a basis for advancement.

4. They must abolish restrictions based on the residence of prospective employees which effectively close the doors to vital talents which may not be locally available.

In short, it is time to rid our local governments of much that typifies what is commonly known as the "career system." There is an urgent need for able men and women who want to devote their lives to progressive growth and achievement in each branch of local government. But such men and women will not be attracted or held by a system that endows the incapable and slothful with a right to permanence in a job, that gears advance for the efficient and inefficient alike to years of service, and that awards a pension after a career of time-serving.

d. *Mobility must be greatly facilitated.* Because many units of local government are too small to offer satisfying careers for talented men and women, ways must be found to stimulate mobility. Two actions by local governments, supplemented by the collaboration of state governments, will facilitate such mobility:

1. The maintenance and use by local governments of a central roster which informs able men and women of job opportunities throughout the country.

2. The establishment of a nation-wide retirement program for local government employees so that the shackles of local retirement systems can be done away with. This action is especially needed.[9]

These actions are not without precedent: professional associations and some universities make possible the mobility of some qualified people; several state-wide training programs make known the capabilities of employees; a few

[9] The U.S. Civil Service Commission has given indications of concern with this approach. John W. Macy, its chairman, has stated that he would set up a study group to develop a "plan to coordinate the many public service retirement systems to facilitate transfers of employees among federal, state, county and city governments."

state-wide retirement systems facilitate mobility. The contract device is well-suited to the loan of personal services for limited periods. Upon these precedents new and more effective devices must be built.

But all of this will not satisfy the future manpower needs of the governments in our metropolitan areas. Most desirable is a national career service which would make careers in local government substantially competitive with those which are available in industry or the federal government.

The opportunity for the individual to move from one local government to another or between levels of government depends not only on transferable retirement provisions. It depends as well on developing standards of professional development that encourage mobility, and on establishing regional and national manpower pools that facilitate exchange of personnel. Professional associations can help, in collaboration with federal, state, and local governments, by working out an effective system for creating regional and national manpower pools to promote interchange of APT personnel.

e. *Recruitment practices must be thoroughly renovated.* With the accomplishment of the previous recommendations, local governments will have taken a giant step forward in providing a more satisfying challenge to able personnel. To compete in the labor market effectively, however, they must adopt more aggressive and enlightened recruiting practices. Such practices are essential so that they may compete with other employers for young people entering their first jobs and so that they may attract able administrative, professional and technical personnel unaccustomed to "working for the government."

Local governments should first undertake long-range manpower planning—three to five years ahead—guided by a personnel agency adequately financed and staffed to recruit with the best techniques, stimulate personal development, and evaluate how well APT people are utilized after they are employed.

Such planning means determining the number of men and women that will be required in the future for each department and in each administrative, professional and technical field.

In order to fill many of these APT positions, the local unit will have to recruit in the national market. Mindful of the keener competition, governing bodies should give the chief executive full support in using whatever devices are needed to find fully qualified personnel. Local units should make fuller use of the national professional associations, state leagues of municipalities, and those universities which provide placement services. Private employment agencies and executive talent scouts are available and often effective.

Local governments must also seek out top college graduates. College recruitment programs must be planned and instituted. Continuing relationships must be built between the urban governments and colleges and universities by informing placement officials and professors of the opportunities open to young people.

In 1962, private businesses stepped up their college recruitment activities by nearly 25 per cent over 1961. The challenge to local government seems clear. As one business personnel analyst writes:

> College recruitment today is big business. More companies are going to more colleges to get more young men. Higher salaries are being offered. Many companies have college relations directors who keep in close contact throughout the year with the schools visited by their companies.[10]

This report has stated repeatedly that urban local governments are growth industries, offering unusual challenges to talented people. At the higher administrative and program levels and in such fields as public health, public welfare, education, and law enforcement, the local official is dealing with the most intriguing and significant problems in modern society; problems whose diversity, complexity and significance demand the highest degree of dedication and community service characteristic of the modern public servant.[11]

5. *Colleges and universities must meet the needs of an urban society.* A rapid expansion of the total supply of APT personnel is fundamentally the role of the colleges and universities. Their output of trained men and women must be promptly and significantly increased. Executives of local governments in every metropolitan area should

---

[10] Stephen Hobbe, "College Recruitment," *Management Record,* January, 1962, p. 28.

[11] See Appendix 2, Careers in the Rebuilding and Management of Cities.

work with colleges and universities to acquaint them with governmental manpower needs and the educational programs that are needed to meet those needs.

The universities can meet this obligation only if they increase the knowledge of urban problems held by their faculties and their students through much more research than is now being done on the metropolitan area, its government, and its myriad problems.[12]

To research and to a rapid expansion of the supply of persons should be added a third and not yet accepted responsibility of educational institutions. Universities, particularly state universities and other universities based in metropolitan areas, must take the lead in helping to close the gap between research completed and application of that research in urban areas. A hopeful beginning is represented in the urban extension programs now under way at Rutgers University and the Universities of Delaware, Wisconsin, Oklahoma and Illinois.

Specifically, the Commission makes these recommendations for action by this country's colleges and universities:

a. *Each should strive to "reach down" to undergraduate students, to introduce these young men and women to the*

---

[12] There is evidence that this challenge is being accepted. In the last ten years, educational institutions in several regions have given increasing emphasis to a study of the process of urbanism and of emerging urban problems. Research projects have been begun in political science, sociology, economics and psychology. Centers of urban studies have been created by cooperative action of leading universities in the Washington, D.C., Boston, and St. Louis metropolitan areas. These activities, although still in their infancy, have already added to our stock of fundamental knowledge about urban affairs. They should be pursued vigorously.

new urban America and to the problems and challenges of a local government career service. The need is to enlist the interests of young people before career choices are made. The systematic infusion of courses on urban affairs in college programs will inform them of career opportunities which they otherwise would not know existed. Thus, it can be expected to attract students from many fields to urban government.

Engineering students, for example, should gain an understanding of the urban economic, social, and political environment in which their professional careers may be pursued. In view of the fact that civil engineering curricula are being revised in many universities throughout the country, the Commission is persuaded that the introduction of courses on urban problems may provide impetus for professional re-orientation of these careers. Similar courses might be introduced in other professional schools.

b. *Universities should seek increased public and private support that they may revise and expand graduate programs which will better equip more students for careers in urban governments.* Special educational programs are needed to devote as much attention to metropolitan problems as a score of outstanding schools of public administration now devote to federal and state activities. This need is especially apparent in the fields of urban renewal, urban transportation, public health, public safety and fiscal management.

If such programs are to be established, new sources of financial aid must be found both for educational institutions and for graduate students. No longer do the bulk of all graduate students pay their own way in higher education; the federal government has already taken steps to increase the supply of graduate students in fields of scientific research, scholarly endeavor, and for federal administrative careers. The same must be done with respect to local government. Fellowships and special grants, established and supported by local government, locally oriented foundations, states and federal government, could awaken interest in local careers. New York's state-wide intern program illustrates such an effort.

c. *The state universities and other institutions of higher education based in metropolitan areas have both an opportunity and an obligation to transmit new knowledge of urban problems to government officials.* Whether universities take on responsibility for post-entry training—and some state universities are developing sound programs for this purpose—they are the proper institutions to help elected and APT officials study in depth long-range problems of urban areas.

In addition to conventional post-entry training, officials must be aided in understanding and interpreting the long-range implications of technology, physical growth, and economic change which are rapidly changing the urban habitat and the services its inhabitants require. They can be aided if the universities will launch broad, continuing urban research programs, and involve the APT personnel of local governments just as fully and successfully as the land grant colleges have worked with farmers and agricultural leaders for a century.

d. *All educational institutions should strive to give greater status and recognition to programs of training for urban careers particularly in professional associations of university administrators, professors and their respective disciplines.* To remedy the neglect of urban matters, special committees in each of these major professional associations should be established. These committees should: (1) Inquire into the state of instruction now offered in urban affairs in their institutions and their fields of knowledge; (2) Identify the deficiencies which exist; (3) Organize plans for improving the extent and quality of the program.

Whenever possible, these committees ought to meet with their counterparts in local government to plan for specific regions and areas. Courses of action can be undertaken to ensure an expanded supply of APT personnel. Because the professional associations themselves are frequently organized on a regional basis, this means of review and evaluation of planning should proceed without delay.

e. Finally, the Commission urges that a national organization be established to assume responsibility for identifying and focusing attention on the major, unsolved problems of urban communities such as the need for total metropolitan planning, for new approaches to metropolitan transportation, for greater understanding of urban renewal and of other social, economic and physical problems.

What is needed in an urban civilization is the analysis and illumination of new and critical problems by some of society's best minds. That need constitutes an unmatched opportunity for the existing associations, the independent research or planning institution, or for a major university.

The Outlook

The vitality of urban America is at this moment one of the most important domestic priorities. Urban public service, staffed by able, interested personnel, can go far to maintain this vitality. If the best talents are not at work to tackle the problems and make the decisions of the metropolitan areas, the daily lives of our urban dwellers will be adversely affected.

The urban resident seeks from his local government education for his children, roads, rapid transit, sanitary facilities, adequate water supply, clear and unpolluted air, police and fire protection, parks and recreation facilities, regulation of utilities "affected with a public interest," and protection from fraud and the unscrupulous.

He needs planning, zoning and tax administration to protect the value of his home, his business and his job. To provide these essentials and others, decisions must recurrently be made on such questions as: Shall there be bridges or tunnels, superhighways or mass transit, better trained police or bigger jails, more money for welfare or for public health?

These decisions will be made for him by people—hopefully the best, the most talented, the most gifted; not the cast-offs, the security seekers, the uninterested.

We conclude our deliberations fully aware of the complexities of local government and the frustrating, bewildering setting within which APT personnel must act. But we are optimistic that, once the problem is thoroughly understood, the state of urban affairs can be substantially improved.

Progress in building a satisfactory human habitat in an urban society will require a consistent team effort. The metropolitan area team involves our citizens, our civic and political leaders on all levels of government, and the APT people in our urban governments. Without this team effort, cities and suburbs will never provide the environment that Americans deserve in which to live, work, and play.

When this team moves in high gear to undertake the actions listed, the American people will be well on their way to achieving the City of Man.

APPENDIX *1*

Municipal Executives:
A Statistical Profile

1. THE MEN WHO ARE MUNICIPAL EXECUTIVES: INTRODUCTION

Where do municipal executives come from? Are they drawn from the higher social and economic families, or are they drawn from all walks of life? More specifically, what was the occupation of their fathers and the education of their parents? How do they compare in origins with business leaders and federal executives?

How are they educated and trained for their positions? How many went to college? What were their areas of specialization in college? How does their educational experience prepare them for their present jobs? Here again, how do municipal executives compare with their counterparts in the federal government and in business?

What are the career routes leading to the position of municipal executive? How many went directly from education to municipal government service? How many served an apprenticeship in private business? How often have they moved from one municipal government to another? How long did it take them to become municipal executives? In what ways are their career patterns similar to and in what ways different from those of leaders in the federal government and in business?

Finally, for what reasons did these executives enter municipal service, and what do they believe they got out of it? Why did they seek an executive position? What do they think of it, in absolute terms and in relation to executive positions elsewhere? Would they enter it again? Would they advise others to do the same thing?

How, by these dimensions, do executives in large cities compare with executives in small cities? How do executives in positions which are different functionally, as engineering or planning in contrast to social welfare, compare? How do executives within civil service systems compare with elected and appointed officials? How do younger and older executives compare?

At the outset of the Municipal Manpower Commission's inquiries the answers to all such questions were lacking. Little or nothing was known about municipal executives as people. Yet to evaluate the manpower now employed by local governments and to foresee the manpower problems ahead, answers to these and related questions were needed. In order to secure the answers, the Commission mailed a questionnaire to 3,000 municipal executives in cities of over 25,000 population.[1] Of those who received the questionnaires, 1,725 replied, a return of 58 per cent. Table 1 shows how those who replied are representative

TABLE 1. EXECUTIVES IN SAMPLE

	All Cities	Cities Over 250,000	Cities Under 250,000
All Executives	1,725	1,054	671
Mayors	28	10	18
City Managers	45	17	28
Assistant Chief Executives	46	22	24
Department Heads	883	505	378
Division Heads	723	500	223
Personnel	77	59	18
Planning	79	52	27
Parks-Recreation	89	47	42
Finance	230	137	93
Health & Welfare	174	119	55
Public Works	483	299	184
Public Safety	220	112	108
Other	254	180	74

of large and smaller American cities and how they are distributed by the positions they fill and the types of jobs they do. Table 2 indicates the response rate by city size and the proportion of the U.S. population living in each size of city.

[1] In particular, this survey was designed to secure information directly comparable to that developed in the following significant and related studies: W. Lloyd Warner and James C. Abegglen, *Occupational Mobility in American Business and Industry* (Minneapolis: University of Minnesota Press, 1955). Warner and Abegglen, *Big Business Leaders in America* (New York: Harper and Brothers, 1952). W. Lloyd Warner, Paul P. Van Riper, Norman H. Martin, and Orvis Collins, *The American Federal Executives* (Conn.: Yale University Press, to be published).

The municipal executives receiving questionnaires included mayors, city managers, chief administrative officers, the chief assistant to the top elected or appointed official, department heads, and division heads.

TABLE 2. RATE OF QUESTIONNAIRE RETURN BY SIZE OF CITY

	Number Mailed	Returned		Per cent of national population living in cities this size
		Number	Per cent	
Executives in:				
Cities over 250,000	1,800	1,054	59	22
Cities under 250,000	1,200	671	56	20
All Cities	3,000	1,725	58	

2. SOCIAL ORIGIN AND EDUCATION

It is at the local level that the actions of government have the most immediate impact on the lives of citizens. If at this level government becomes a bureaucracy staffed by a caste-like class of men handing power down through the generations, then citizens may indeed be annoyed by and resist the demands placed upon them by their governments. If the search for new executives is restricted to sons of highly placed men, then much of the talent reservoir of the country goes untapped. Further, if the men who assume positions of leadership in municipal government are not adequately trained and selected, then municipal government can at best be only partially effective and efficient. In this chapter we examine the social origins of municipal executives and the formal training which is their basic equipment for performing their key functions.

Occupational Origins

What are the proportions of municipal executives recruited from the different social classes? For our purposes
occupation is the best indication of social class. Table 3
shows the occupations of the fathers of municipal and
business executives.

TABLE 3. FATHERS' OCCUPATIONS

	Municipal Executives	Business Leaders *
Clerk	6%	2%
Salesman	7	6
Farmer	11	9
Laborer	30	15
Professional	13	14
Government or Business Executive, or Business Owner	31	52
Unknown	2	2
Total	100%	100%

* Warner and Abegglen, *Occupational Mobility in
American Business and Industry,* op. cit., p. 38.

The majority of municipal executives are drawn from
the non-professional and non-executive occupational
groups. Fifty-four per cent reported that their fathers were
laborers, farmers, or clerks and salesmen. On the other
hand, 44 per cent of municipal executives reported their
fathers were in professional, executive and business owner
categories.

Two facts stand out:

Given the proportions of the national population at the

time when these men's fathers were occupationally engaged, sons of men from the higher occupational levels are over-represented among municipal leaders. Warner and Abegglen report that 15 per cent of the adult males in the national population in 1920 (about ten years after these executives were born) were business owners, executives, or professional men.[2] The municipal executives report 44 per cent of their fathers fell into this category. Dividing 15 per cent into 44 per cent, we find that the proportions of sons of fathers in these occupations are about three times greater than would have been expected on the basis of the national population in 1920. Sons of men from the higher occupational levels are clearly over-represented among municipal executives.

The second fact, and this is of great importance, is that over half the men in the municipal executive positions are not from these elite occupational groups. In 1920 laborers, salesmen or clerks, and farmers combined made up 84 per cent of the total adult male population.[3] Dividing 84 per cent into 54 per cent, we see that the resulting ratio is .64. This means that for every hundred men we would expect to be drawn from these lower occupational groups, only 64 are. While sons of men in the less prestigeful occupations are under-represented in terms of national population, they are far from being excluded from assuming positions of leadership in municipal governments.

[2] Warner and Abegglen, *Occupational Mobility in American Business and Industry*, op. cit., p. 46.
[3] *Ibid.*, p. 22.

The pattern is, then, one of recruiting more than expected from the higher occupational groups, but with the larger proportion of jobs being held by men from the "common man" level. This, with some variations, follows the pattern reported by other studies of recruitment into federal executive positions and into the ranks of ownership and administration of the nation's large businesses. In general, municipal and federal career executives have risen more often from the lower and lower middle occupational levels than have business executives or federal political executives.[4] Business and federal political executives are more often drawn from the professions and from the executive levels. In all these executive groups there is a pattern of occupational prestige being transmitted through the generations; but always with a flow of new people from the lower occupational levels.

Education: Training and Qualification

As the levels of technical and professional skills increase, higher education becomes increasingly both the medium through which men receive training and the gateway through which they must pass to achieve high occupational status. In equipping themselves for movement into municipal executive positions, these men necessarily far outstripped their parents in the levels of education achieved. Table 4 tells the story of this dramatic shift. Only 13 per

[4] For information on the social backgrounds of federal executives, see W. Lloyd Warner, Paul P. Van Riper, Norman H. Martin, and Orvis F. Collins, "Profiles of Government Executives," *Business Topics* (Autumn, 1961), pp. 15, 16.

cent of the executives' fathers and 7 per cent of their mothers were college graduates, but 59 per cent of the executives themselves had graduated from college and an additional 20 per cent attended college but did not graduate.

TABLE 4. EDUCATION: MUNICIPAL EXECUTIVES AND THEIR PARENTS

	Father	Mother	Municipal Executives
High School or Less	78%	83%	21%
Some College	9	10	20
College Graduate	13	7	59

The demand for higher education placed on municipal executives is highly similar to that placed on men entering other administrative fields. Table 5 shows that the educational levels of municipal executives are almost identical to those of business leaders. Eighty per cent of municipal

TABLE 5. EDUCATION OF MUNICIPAL, BUSINESS, AND FEDERAL EXECUTIVES

			Federal	
	Municipal	Business	Career Civil Service	Political Appointees
Attended College	80%	76%	90%	97%
College Graduates	59	57	80	90
Graduate Degrees	25	*	45	75

* Data not available.

SOURCE: *Business Executives:* W. Lloyd Warner and James C. Abegglen, *Occupational Mobility in American Business and Industry* (Minneapolis: University of Minneapolis, 1955), p. 96. *Federal Executives:* W. Lloyd Warner, Paul P. Van Riper, Norman H. Martin, Orvis F. Collins, "Profiles of Government Executives," *Business Topics* (Autumn, 1961), pp. 16, 17. Figures on graduate degrees held by federal executives may be high since some may hold two or more graduate degrees and were counted more than once.

executives attended college, compared with 76 per cent of the business leaders. Although federal executives were somewhat more highly educated than either municipal or business executives, the federal executive figures only underscore the importance of higher education. Further, a fourth of municipal executives, almost half the federal career executives, and three-fourths of the federal political executives have secured advanced degrees. Higher education is, and this is becoming more and more true, the prime qualification for movement into all these administrative positions. Also, higher education is now more commonly defined as holding a four year or advanced degree—not merely having attended college.

Among municipal executives themselves, men holding positions in the larger cities have, on the whole, higher levels of education than men holding positions in the smaller cities. Table 6 shows that 65 per cent of the executives from cities of over 250,000 population reported they were college graduates, compared to 49 per cent in the cities of less than 250,000. Larger proportions of large city executives than small city executives in health, parks and recreation, finance, public works, public safety, and welfare hold four year degrees.

At the graduate degree level the difference between cities over and cities under 250,000 is quite pronounced. Thirty per cent of all executives in the larger cities hold graduate degrees, but only 18 per cent of executives in the smaller cities hold such degrees. Examination of the functional areas shows that 91 per cent of the directors of health in the larger cities hold advanced degrees compared with only 56 per cent of their colleagues in the smaller cities. For directors of welfare the proportions are 55 per cent to 11 per cent, for planning 42 per cent to 27 per cent. The cities over 250,000 are clearly attracting and holding larger proportions of men with advanced training.

TABLE 6. COLLEGE GRADUATES: PROPORTIONS OF MEN HOLDING FOUR YEAR AND ADVANCED DEGREES BY TYPE OF POSITION HELD

	Four Year Degrees		Advanced Degrees	
	Cities 250,000 and over	Cities 250,000 and under	Cities 250,000 and over	Cities 250,000 and under
All Executives	65%	49%	30	18
Managers	82	89	29	33
Department Heads	68	50	34	19
Personnel	68	87	30	20
Planning	85	82	42	27
Parks-Recreation	84	64	32	14
Finance	52	36	20	11
Health	100	72	91	56
Public Works	61	48	16	4
Public Safety	33	11	13	3
Welfare	86	67	55	11
Division Heads	62	38	26	12

Qualification for advancement into areas such as public safety, public works and finance does not demand a college degree, in either large or small cities. In these crucial areas the executive levels are in the majority of cases manned by men with less formal education than their counterparts in other functional areas.

Less than 50 per cent of the men in five categories are college graduates. Two thirds of all directors of public safety in large cities are not college graduates, and about nine out of ten such officials in small cities did not earn a four year degree. In the smaller cities slightly less than half of the directors of public works and slightly more than a third of the directors of finance and of the division heads are college graduates.

Municipal Executives Took Specialized Training in College

Municipal executives are selected for their present executive positions on the basis of narrow technical proficiency rather than on the basis of formal training in administration or in the social science fields such as political science, economics, or sociology. This is true at both the graduate and undergraduate levels. Examining Table 7 we see that,

TABLE 7. COLLEGE DEGREES: FIELDS OF SPECIALIZATION *

	Undergraduate	Graduate
Physical Sciences–Engineering	46%	23%
Professional	11	45
Environmental	26	10
Administration	13	20
Other	4	2
	100%	100%

* The fields are defined as:
  Physical Sciences–Engineering: Engineering, physical sciences, mathematics, planning, architecture, medicine
  Professional: Accounting, library science, physical education, recreation, education, journalism, law
  Environmental: Economics, political science, government, sociology, history, philosophy, psychology, English, languages
  Administration: Public administration, business administration

at the four year level, 57 per cent of these executives received training either in the technical or in the narrowly defined professional fields, but that only 26 per cent received degrees in more general fields such as the humanities and the social sciences. Further, only 13 per cent received degrees in public and business administration.

At the graduate level, concentration in the technical fields is even more extreme. Municipal executives took 68 per cent of their advanced degrees in technical and professional fields, with 23 per cent concentrating in the technical and 45 per cent in the professional. Specialization in the administrative areas was increased only from 13 per cent to 20 per cent. The proportion of men who received training in the broad environmental—social science—fields dropped from 26 per cent to 10 per cent. Does this mean that the municipal executive force suffers from imbalance toward technical training?

Looking behind the broad categories, we find a partial answer to this question. We see in Table 8 that men with technical degrees at the four year level are heavily concentrated in certain functional areas. Over three-fourths of all holders of four year degrees in public works and in health took their degrees in physical sciences–engineering, and 70 per cent of planning officials hold a degree in this area. By contrast about two-thirds of the welfare directors took environmental subject degrees, and among finance directors 42 per cent of degree holders earned their degrees in business administration.

TABLE 8. COLLEGE DEGREE FIELDS BY FUNCTIONAL AREA OF POSITION

	Physical Sciences * Engineering	Professional †	Environmental	Administration	Other	Total
Undergraduate						
Managers	41%	6%	23%	30%	—%	100%
Department Heads	45	9	27	14	5	100
Personnel	13	8	50	26	3	100
Planning	70	—	19	11	—	100
Parks-Rec.	38	47	12	3	—	100
Finance	15	13	22	46	4	100
Health	78	—	6	8	8	100
Pub. Works	85	1	6	5	3	100
Pub. Safety	23	11	32	28	6	100
Welfare	17	13	66	—	4	100
Division Heads	52	13	21	9	5	100
Graduate						
Managers	20%	7%	—%	73%	—%	100%
Department Heads	24	49	9	15	3	100
Personnel	—	43	36	21	—	100
Planning	70	10	10	10	—	100
Parks-Rec.	20	70	—	—	10	100
Finance	5	66	5	24	—	100
Health	47	—	3	50	—	100
Pub. Works	61	39	—	—	—	100
Pub. Safety	22	67	11	—	—	100
Welfare	7	14	65	14	—	100
Division Heads	24	44	11	18	3	100

* On the graduate level, the physical sciences include medical degrees. However, if a person holds both an M.D. and a masters of public health or public administration, this person was included under "Administration." Virtually all health directors with masters degrees in administration (normally MPH) have M.D.'s as well.

† Includes law on the graduate level.

Education and Career

The increasing importance of higher education as qualification for entrance into municipal executive positions is
shown by Chart 8. Over two-thirds of men under fifty years,
but only half the men over fifty years, have four year

CHART 8

Age and Education of Municipal Executives

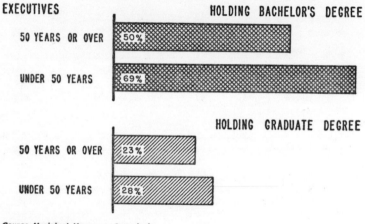

EXECUTIVES   HOLDING BACHELOR'S DEGREE

50 YEARS OR OVER   50%

UNDER 50 YEARS   69%

                                              HOLDING GRADUATE DEGREE

50 YEARS OR OVER   23%

UNDER 50 YEARS   28%

Source: Municipal Manpower Commission

degrees. Again, 28 per cent of the men under fifty, while
23 per cent of the men over fifty, hold advanced degrees.

Is this development the result of civil service rules re-
quiring higher education as an entrance qualification? We
can get a partial answer by comparing proportions of men
with college degrees within the civil service systems with
those men in positions exempt from civil service requirements. Chart 9, which presents this comparison, discloses

that slightly higher proportions of men appointed and elected to their positions than men within the civil service systems have taken college degrees, at both the four year

CHART 9

Education of Civil Service and Political Executives

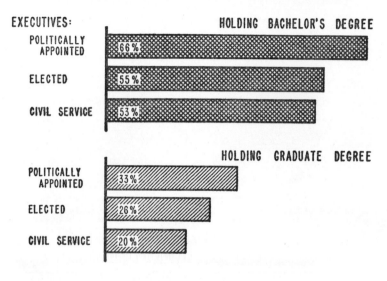

EXECUTIVES: HOLDING BACHELOR'S DEGREE

POLITICALLY
APPOINTED   66%

ELECTED   55%

CIVIL SERVICE   53%

HOLDING GRADUATE DEGREE

POLITICALLY
APPOINTED   33%

ELECTED   26%

CIVIL SERVICE   20%

Source: Municipal Manpower Commission

and advanced levels. This strongly suggests that qualification for appointment or election to high municipal office today requires more formal education than does movement into the high civil service positions.

3. CAREERS AND CAREER PATTERNS

A man's total career spans the time between his completing formal education and his present age. For municipal executives, career spans may be thought of as falling into four major periods. These are (1) the period after completing formal education but before entering a local government, (2) the period between entering a local government and entering the particular government in which a man is now employed, (3) the period between entering his present government and achieving his present position, and (4) the period between the executive's assuming his present position and the executive's present age.

Assuming that the majority of these executives have followed such an orderly progression, but keeping in mind that many have not, we have in Chart 10 plotted the average years spent by executives in larger cities in each of the four major career periods. In Chart 11, mindful that important differences have emerged between executives in the larger and executives in the smaller cities, we have plotted the average career periods for executives in smaller cities. These two charts are the skeletons for the examination of career mobility into high municipal position.

The "average" executive waited nine years after leaving school to enter local government employment. Three years later he first joined his present government and reached executive level in nine years. He has been in his present position for seven years.

A first glance at Charts 10 and 11 shows that length of career span varies by kinds of positions. The career spans of planning executives, for example, are relatively short— 21 years in large and 18 years in small cities—compared

CHART 10

Municipal Executives' Career Patterns: Average Time Spent in Four Major Periods (Large Cities)

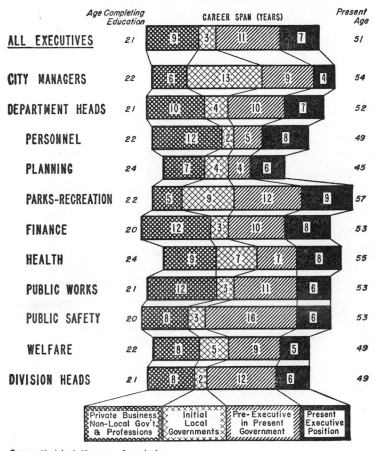

	Age Completing Education	CAREER SPAN (YEARS)	Present Age
ALL EXECUTIVES	21	9 3 11 7	51
CITY MANAGERS	22	6 13 9 4	54
DEPARTMENT HEADS	21	10 4 10 7	52
PERSONNEL	22	12 2 5 8	49
PLANNING	24	7 4 4 6	45
PARKS-RECREATION	22	5 9 12 9	57
FINANCE	20	12 3 10 8	53
HEALTH	24	9 7 7 8	55
PUBLIC WORKS	21	12 3 11 6	53
PUBLIC SAFETY	20	8 3 16 6	53
WELFARE	22	8 5 9 5	49
DIVISION HEADS	21	8 2 12 6	49

Private Business, Non-Local Gov't, & Professions | Initial Local Governments | Pre-Executive in Present Government | Present Executive Position

Source: Municipal Manpower Commission

143

CHART 11

Municipal Executives' Career Patterns: Average Time Spent in Four Major Periods (Small Cities)

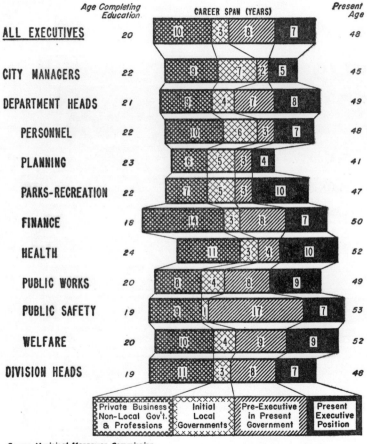

Source: Municipal Manpower Commission

with public safety executives who have had 33-year spans
in large and 34-year spans in small cities. These substantial
variations suggest that there are distinctive career problems
in different functional areas.

From Formal Education to First Local Government

Charts 10 and 11 show that municipal executives in
large cities left school at an average age of twenty-one, those
in smaller cities at twenty. In one functional area, executives finished formal education at eighteen and the members of another at an average age of twenty-four. Table 9
indicates that in both large and small cities these men were

TABLE 9. AGE FIRST ENTERING LOCAL GOVERNMENT

	Cities	
	Over 250,000	Under 250,000
Executives by City Size	30	30
Managers	28	31
Chief Assistants	31	29
Department Heads	32	30
Personnel	34	30
Planning	30	29
Parks-Recreation	27	28
Finance	32	32
Health	33	35
Public Works	33	29
Public Safety	27	27
Welfare	29	30
Division Heads	29	30
All Executives	30	

on the average 30 years old when they first entered local
government employment. There was, then, a period of
nine years transition between leaving school and entering

local government. Table 9 also shows us that the range between the oldest and youngest by functional category entering local government was eight years.

During the period before they came into local government, as Table 10 shows, about half the municipal executives were in private business. Relatively, only a handful were in professional practice or in state or federal government. The majority of those men who did not first go into private business moved directly into local government.

The movement into private business or into government varies significantly with area of functional specialization. Personnel and finance directors started in private business much more often than the average executive. Even city managers and public safety directors started largely in non-local government employment. Such specialized men as parks-recreation and health directors were more inclined to begin their careers in local government than in private business, although one-third of the health directors started in their own professional practice.

In certain functional areas, smaller cities appear to be getting more executives trained for local government service. Personnel directors in small cities were much less likely than their large city counterparts to begin careers in private business. The small city personnel director is just as likely to have come to local government from state or federal employment as he is from private business. Small city personnel directors appear better prepared— educationally—for their work than do those in large cities.

TABLE 10. MUNICIPAL EXECUTIVES: THEIR CAREER STARTS

	First Employer						
	Private Business	Local Government	Federal Government	State Government	Profession	Other	All
All Executives	51%	25%	7%	6%	5%	6%	100%
Cities over 250,000	50	25	7	6	5	7	100
Cities under 250,000	51	25	8	5	5	6	100
All Cities							
Managers	55	20	4	14	5	2	100
Department Heads	48	25	9	5	7	6	100
Personnel	62	16	8	10	—	4	100
Planning	38	27	12	13	6	4	100
Parks-Rec.	24	45	9	2	2	18	100
Finance	69	20	7	—	3	1	100
Health	18	20	13	7	33	9	100
Public Works	50	26	10	9	2	3	100
Public Safety	57	23	8	1	4	7	100
Welfare	40	27	—	10	10	13	100
Division Heads	55	20	4	14	5	2	100

Those in smaller cities emphasized public administration, political science and psychology.

City managers in small cities began more often in local government than did those in similar positions in large units. Similarly it appears that those in smaller cities prepare themselves educationally for local government employment to a greater extent than do those in larger cities. In small cities, managers are more apt to have majored in political science or public administration, on both graduate and undergraduate levels, than their counterparts in large cities.

Although half of all present municipal executives began their careers in private business, Table 11 suggests sig-

TABLE 11. FIRST EMPLOYER BY PRESENT AGE

	Under 40	40–55	Over 55
Local Government	30%	21%	27%
Other Government (state and federal)	23	11	10
Private business	37	58	48
Other (prof. practice, farmer, organization)	11	10	15
	100%	100%	100%

nificant differences when the ages of executives are considered. Men aged 40–55, in much larger percentages than either younger or older men, were first employed in private business. On the other hand, a smaller percentage of men in this age bracket started in local government. This suggests that recruitment during the time when age group 40–55 came into local government had special circumstances not found at earlier and later periods.

Table 12 divides municipal executives into four decades of entry. Notable is the fact that today's municipal executives moved in at a fairly constant rate during the four decades.

TABLE 12. PERIOD DURING WHICH PRESENT MUNICIPAL EXECUTIVES FIRST ENTERED LOCAL GOVERNMENT

Period	Per cent Entered	Cumulative
1930 or before	22%	22%
1931–40	25	47
1941–50	24	71
1951–61	29	100
	100%	

Movement between Local Governments

The average executive did not enter local government until nine years after completing formal schooling. Once entering, however, there was a pronounced tendency to stay in the same government. Despite an average of three years spent moving between units, over three-fourths of all executives, Table 13 shows, have worked for only one city. This holds for almost every category of executive, regardless of size of city. Only in the cases of city managers and directors of planning have less than 50 per cent stayed with their initial local government. Less than ten per cent of all municipal executives have changed units more than twice.

It appears that business leaders have tended to move much more often from firm to firm than municipal executives from local government to local government. Warner and Abegglen report only 25 per cent of business leaders have stayed with their original firm.[5] It must, however, be borne in mind that over half of the municipal executives moved into local government following an earlier career in either private business or in a state or the federal government.

TABLE 13. MOBILITY OF MUNICIPAL EXECUTIVES

| | Number of Local Governments Worked for | | | | |
	1	2	3	4 or more	All
All Executives	81%	13%	4%	2%	100%
Managers	34	13	16	37	100
Department Heads	78	14	5	3	100
Personnel	80	14	6	0	100
Planning	48	29	9	14	100
Parks-Recreation	59	15	17	9	100
Finance	81	17	1	1	100
Health	72	26	2	0	100
Public Works	80	14	4	2	100
Public Safety	90	7	2	1	100
Welfare	85	12	2	1	100
Division Heads	85	12	2	1	100

From Entrance to Present Position

The average executive took nine years to achieve his present position after entering his present government. Public safety directors took the longest—sixteen years in large cities and seventeen years in smaller—to reach the top of their career ladders. At the other extreme, managers of small cities spent an average of only two years in a non-city manager post after entering their government. Planning and personnel directors also moved up rapidly, taking only three to five years.

[5] W. Lloyd Warner, Paul P. Van Riper, Norman H. Martin, and Orvis F. Collins, "Profiles of Government Executives," *Business Topics* (Autumn, 1961), p. 127.

These wide variations clearly reflect a substantial difference between certain fields for which lateral entry is the
pattern and other fields in which executives are promoted
from within. Table 14 distinguishes between these different areas. About one half of the managers, chief assistants,

TABLE 14. PROPORTION OF EXECUTIVES RECEIVING DIRECT
APPOINTMENT FROM OTHER EMPLOYMENT TO PRESENT
POSITION AND PROPORTIONS HAVING HAD PREVIOUS
GOVERNMENT EXPERIENCE

	All	
	Proportion Appointed Directly	Have Had Previous L.G. Experience
Executives (All)	35%	83%
Managers	53	87
Department Heads	39	82
Personnel	52	73
Planning	49	86
Parks-Recreation	53	83
Finance	35	84
Health	52	81
Public Works	36	83
Public Safety	19	89
Welfare	36	87
Division Heads	28	85

and directors of personnel, planning, parks-recreation and
health were directly appointed into their present positions.
These are the professions which increasingly require
specialized academic training. For these functional fields,
professional men tend to be sought, and in these fields
there is more frequent lateral entry.

Despite the high percentage of lateral entry, however,
men without local government experience are not usually

CHART 12

Top Executive Posts Are Filled Largely from within Same Government (Proportion of Executives Who Held Other Positions in Present Government)

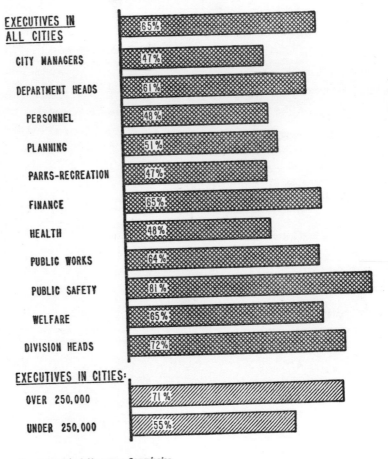

EXECUTIVES IN ALL CITIES — 65%

CITY MANAGERS — 47%

DEPARTMENT HEADS — 61%

PERSONNEL — 48%

PLANNING — 51%

PARKS-RECREATION — 47%

FINANCE — 65%

HEALTH — 48%

PUBLIC WORKS — 64%

PUBLIC SAFETY — 81%

WELFARE — 65%

DIVISION HEADS — 72%

EXECUTIVES IN CITIES:

OVER 250,000 — 71%

UNDER 250,000 — 55%

Source: Municipal Manpower Commission

appointed into these high positions. An apprenticeship is served either in the same or in another local government.

Chart 12 shows that over half of executives in small cities and about 70 per cent of executives in large cities were promoted from within. This suggests that smaller cities may be freer than larger cities to recruit widely for high level personnel. When we look at positions within functional fields for both large and small cities, we see that less than half the city managers and directors of personnel, parks-recreation and health were appointed from within. Because of the special training and experience required for these positions, the cities do go outside to meet their recruitment needs.

Many Executives Are Covered by Civil Service

Very few executives in the study—only 10 per cent—were in cities lacking formal civil service systems. Table 15 compares the means by which executives were chosen for their positions and the nature of the position. Of department heads, only 7 per cent were elected—largely in the function of finance, where one in four directors is chosen by the voter. Thus, more than 90 per cent of directors were appointed, rather than elected, to their present posts.

What is the nature of their appointment? In cities with civil service systems, nearly 40 per cent of the directors are covered by civil service provisions. This tendency is more pronounced in smaller cities, but even in larger cities one-third of all department heads are covered. Public safety and personnel directors have the highest degree of civil

TABLE 15. NATURE OF PRESENT POSITION

	Appointed			Elected	Total
	Civil Service	Exempt from Civil Service	No Civil Serv. in City		
All Executives	46%	39%	10%	5%	100%
Cities over 250,000	48	42	6	4	100
Cities under 250,000	42	34	16	8	100
Dept. Heads (All Cities)	31	50	11	7	100
Personnel	44	48	8	—	100
Planning	40	46	15	—	100
Parks-Rec.	30	47	15	9	100
Finance	20	52	5	24	100
Health	31	54	13	2	100
Pub. Works	28	56	15	2	100
Pub. Safety	49	34	12	4	100
Welfare	35	58	7	—	100
Division Heads	70	21	8	—	100

service coverage at this level of responsibility; division heads, however, are even more likely to be in covered positions.

Tenure of Municipal Executives

The most revealing aspects of Table 16 are that (1) municipal executives have a relatively long tenure—or at least

TABLE 16. YEARS IN PRESENT POSITION

	Cities Over 250,000	Cities Under 250,000
All Executives	7	7
Department Heads	7	8
Division Heads	6	7
All Executives—All Cities	7	

they are not replaced as often as might be assumed since many are subject to "political" appointment and removal and (2) department heads, with markedly less civil service coverage than division heads, have held their positions longer.

Age and Retirement

The average age of large city executives is fifty-one; in smaller cities, the average is forty-eight. Combined, municipal executives are fifty years old, on the average. Health and public safety directors are the oldest and planning directors by far the youngest. Table 17 shows that retire-

TABLE 17. PRESENT AGES OF MUNICIPAL EXECUTIVES

	Present Age	
	Over 250,000	Under 250,000
All Executives	51	48
Managers-CAO	54	45
Department Heads	52	49
Personnel	49	48
Planning	45	41
Parks-Recreation	57	47
Finance	53	50
Health	55	52
Public Works	53	49
Public Safety	53	53
Welfare	49	52
Division Heads	49	48
All Executives—All Cities	50	

ment of municipal executives is a problem increasingly to be faced.

More than one-third of all municipal executives are within a decade of retirement age. One-fifth will reach sixty-five within five years, 6 per cent have already reached or passed retirement age and 2 per cent are seventy or over. The significance of age is further heightened in some critical functional areas. Half the health directors will be eligible for retirement in ten years, and one in four in five years. Virtually the same is true for parks-recreation directors; well above average retirement rates are also found among public works, public safety and finance directors.

TABLE 18. AGE DISTRIBUTION

	Under 40	40–44	45–49	50–54	55–59	Over 60	Totals
Executives in							
All Cities	19%	13%	15%	19%	16%	18%	100%
Managers	22	18	11	18	18	13	100
Depart. Heads	16	13	15	18	18	20	100
Personnel	22	13	19	15	15	16	100
Planning	34	20	22	9	11	4	100
Parks-Rec.	15	13	9	17	26	20	100
Finance	12	18	13	18	15	24	100
Health	8	6	6	30	25	25	100
Pub. Works	18	12	15	12	19	24	100
Pub. Safety	9	5	19	27	15	25	100
Welfare	3	16	23	26	16	16	100
Division Heads	21	12	16	20	15	16	100

Noteworthy is the fact revealed in Table 18 that division heads are about the same age as departments heads. They will not provide a sure reservoir of promotional material due to their own approaching retirement.

Summary

Now aged fifty, the average municipal executive has been in his current position an average of seven years. At the peak of his career, he is well seasoned by experience to deal with his locality's problems.

Beneath this hopeful "average" picture are several clear and important points which emerge from the data on careers presented in this section.

First, municipal executives are twice as likely to start their careers in private business than in local government. Their period of non-local government employment extends nine years before they first enter the municipal public service.

Second, the overwhelming majority of municipal executives have worked for only one local government. This contrasts sharply with the mobility found among business executives, one-fourth of whom have worked for only one firm.

Third, many municipal executives are approaching retirement: more than one-third are fifty-five or older, and nearly one out of five is already within five years of retirement.

4. MOTIVATION AND ATTITUDES

Motivation and satisfaction are subtle and complex factors. A national survey based on the answers to mailed questionnaires can yield only crude measures of such factors. Yet, the responses of a representative sample of local officials do provide a starting point.

Why Did They Go into Local Government?

Why are today's executives in local government? Did they come in because no other suitable job was available? Did they wish an opportunity for public service? The range of responses in Table 19 indicates that general career perspectives—as opposed to specific considerations such as salary and retirement benefits—were most important to initial entry. If we look at these categories in terms of percentages of executives choosing each category as a primary response, we find that 40 per cent chose the category "general nature of the work." This is in a sense a general and non-committal response. The positive response "op-

TABLE 19. WHY DID EXECUTIVES ENTER LOCAL GOVERNMENT?

Factor	Given as Primary Reason	Mentioned Most Frequently (Rank)
General nature of the work	40%	1
Opportunity to help solve public problems	13	3
Only position available in your line of work	11	8
Opportunity for advancement	10	2
Job security	8	6
Salary	7	4
Important Responsibility	4	5
Good experience for entering private business	3	10
Prestige	1	7
Political opportunities	1	13
Retirement benefits	1	9
Low pressure	*	14
Other fringe benefits (not retirement)	*	12
Co-workers	*	11

* Less than one per cent.

portunity to help solve public problems" and the negative response "only position available in your line of work" both received about ten per cent of the first responses. This indicates conflicting motivations.

One executive who checked "only position available" as his reason for entering local government added, "In 1938, the scarcity of positions made many other factors unimportant." Another executive, who entered local government during the early 1950's, candidly said, "I was a failure while employed by private industry." A division head commented that "private employment prejudice" at the time of the Korean War forced him into local government. One executive stated that there was no other position open in his home town. Another remarked, "... this job involves no cross-country travel and allows me to live at home." A department head was "... tired of living out of a suitcase." These comments indicate a wide range of motivations.

Motivation for entry was affected by economic and social trends outside municipal government (see Table 20). "Se-

TABLE 20. DEPRESSION VS. RECENT ENTRANTS

Period	Proportion Entered in Period	Entered Because of "Only Position Available" or "Security"
1930 or before	22%	22%
1931–1940	25	29
1941–1945	8	19
1946–1955	30	12
1956–present	15	8
	100%	

curity" and "only position available" were more important during the depression years. Only 8 per cent of executives who entered since 1956 gave this response. Executives no longer appear to regard themselves as being "forced" into local government. On the whole, evidence indicates that the younger executives entering since World War II are better qualified educationally and more often have entered local government as a matter of choice.

Table 19 further suggests that salary and prestige were relatively minor primary influences on the executives, and that political opportunity was also unimportant. This is contrary to the often-expressed opinion that "politics" control the appointment of local officials. On the other hand, with only about one in five entering for either the opportunity to help solve public problems or opportunity for advancement, these motives lagged well behind the general nature of the work as an attraction. Finally, it is clear that retirement and other fringe benefits had negligible influence in the choice.

Why They Accepted Executive Positions

Municipal executives accepted their present position for more definite and positive reasons than those given for first entering local government. For example, executives in accepting their present position were much more influenced by the opportunity to help in the solution of public problems. Over one-fifth of these executives accepted their post primarily because of their interest in solving public problems, and ten per cent cited "important responsibilities."

Salary and opportunities for advancement were also a relatively significant primary factor in attracting these executives to their present positions.

Prestige and advancement opportunity do not rank significantly high among the major reasons municipal executives accepted their present positions.

TABLE 21. WHY EXECUTIVES ACCEPTED PRESENT POSITION

Rank	Factor	Given as Primary Reason	Factors Mentioned Most Frequently (Rank)
1	General nature of the work	31%	1
2	Opportunity to help solve public problems	21	3
3	Important responsibilities	10	2
4	Salary	11	4
5	Opportunity for advancement	10	6
6	Prestige	3	5
7	Only position available in your line of work	2	13
8	Job security	2	7
9	Good experience for entrance into priv. bus.	1	9
10	Political opportunity	1	12
11	Retirement benefits	*	8
12	Other fringe benefits	*	1
13	Congenial co-workers	*	10
14	Low degree of pressure	*	14

* Less than one per cent.

What Do They Think of Public Service Now?

Data in Table 22 suggest that the effect of the prestige of employment in local government must be carefully evaluated. What seems to frustrate municipal executives is an "image" that surrounds the employee of city government. Their responses show that there is a sizable minority

opinion that prestige would be higher in other employment—whether private business, local or national, or government, state or federal. Several respondents expressed
resentment at prevailing public attitudes, citing the terms

TABLE 22. PRESTIGE IN OTHER EMPLOYMENT

Employer	Prestige Would Be:			
	Higher	Same	Lower	Total
Federal Government	32%	47%	21%	100%
State Government	29	55	16	100
Private Business (National)	33	40	27	100
Private Business (Local)	26	43	31	100

"slacker," "loafer," "political hack" or "incompetent" as
too often applied to local public servants.

The sources of dissatisfaction listed by municipal executives are shown in Table 23. It is most significant that
practically none of these men felt their jobs lacked opportunity to solve public problems, and that prestige was not
a source of dissatisfaction. These men concentrated on
economic matters such as salary, advancement opportunities, and fringe benefits as their sources of dissatisfaction.

TABLE 23. SOURCES OF DISSATISFACTION
TO MUNICIPAL EXECUTIVES

Factor	Rank
Salary	1
Advancement opportunities	2
Fringe Benefits (not retirement)	3
Job Security	4
Retirement Benefits	5

The salary level was criticized the most by these executives. As Chart 13 shows, nearly nine out of ten executives felt their salary would be higher if they were working in

CHART 13

Proportion of Municipal Executives Who Indicate Their Salary Would Be Higher in Other Employment

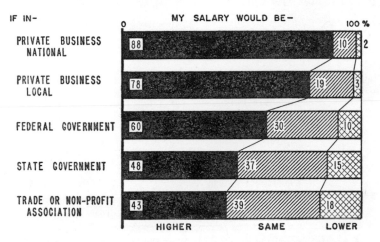

IF IN—   MY SALARY WOULD BE—

PRIVATE BUSINESS NATIONAL: 88 | 10 | 2
PRIVATE BUSINESS LOCAL: 78 | 19 | 3
FEDERAL GOVERNMENT: 60 | 30 | 10
STATE GOVERNMENT: 48 | 37 | 15
TRADE OR NON-PROFIT ASSOCIATION: 43 | 39 | 18

HIGHER   SAME   LOWER

Source: Municipal Manpower Commission

similar positions in a national firm. Three-fourths thought their salary would be higher in a local business enterprise, 60 per cent in the federal government, and between 40 and 50 per cent in a state or non-profit association position.

Current Attitudes toward Local Government Employment

As Table 24 indicates, only 17 per cent of all executives would recommend local government employment to their own sons or daughters, or to a close friend. Over 70 per cent would recommend private business.

The reasons for this overwhelming preference toward private business are not perfectly clear. It appears that low prestige of public employment—interpreted narrowly —does not rank as one of the most significant reasons. The reasons most frequently mentioned in comments attached to questionnaires involve (1) salary and (2) lack of recognition for a job well done—or the opportunity to move up on the basis of merit.

TABLE 24. MUNICIPAL EXECUTIVES'
EMPLOYER PREFERENCE FOR THEIR CHILDREN

Private Business	72%
Local Government	17
Federal Government	8
State Government	2
Trade or Non-profit Association	1
	100%

A small city division head said: "From a purely monetary standpoint, I believe private business would appeal to many as more satisfactory."

Another in a large city explained, "Salary is insufficient to provide the sources from which I can obtain growth as an individual. It is for this reason that I cannot and will not recommend the public service to my son." A New England department head complained, "Governments do not value the services, particularly of professional employees, sufficiently to set a standard of salaries commensurate with the importance and responsibilities of the position. If I had to do it over again, I would never become affiliated with a governmental job on the municipal, state or federal levels."

A waterworks superintendent remarked, "Because of low pay and its inherent frustrations, I would not advise anyone entering public service without a sense of dedication to it."

Another stated, "Private enterprises more readily recognize and reward the individual with initiative. Government is more apt to penalize through civil service yardsticks, categorizing and regimentation."

A large city division head observes, "Time after time, I have seen young engineers allowed to leave the service of the municipal government, simply because they feel that to remain any longer, they would not be allowed to show their initiative."

A Paradox

The municipal executive presents a puzzling, even contradictory accumulation of facts and attitudes. He is generally satisfied with his position, but he is not too happy with his salary and advancement opportunities. He is generally satisfied with the estimation in which he is held by his community, but he is disturbed by the public's image of local government employees. He enjoys the general nature of his work and the challenge of public problems, yet he would seldom advise his son to seek a career in municipal government.

This mixed picture of attitudes does not answer the

question, "Is the municipal executive really satisfied with his job and his employer?" The data on career patterns however, indicate an overwhelming preference to stay in a single city's employment. It must be assumed that the personal satisfaction of these executives outweighs whatever factors cause them to hesitate to encourage younger people to choose local government as a life's career.

This Profile has answered many questions; it has also raised new and more perplexing ones. Like all basic research, it has taken a step forward and should stimulate broader and deeper probes into the nature of the municipal executive.

APPENDIX 2

Excerpts from
"Careers in the Rebuilding and
Management of Cities" [1]

Tens of thousands of important and interesting technical
and professional positions in urban affairs are now open
throughout the country. The present supply of persons
with essential technical and professional education can
meet only a small fraction of the demand. The backlog
of unsatisfied needs indicates that for years to come, the
talented young men or women who prepare for municipal

---

[1] This appendix presents excerpts from a handbook entitled *Careers in
the Rebuilding and Management of Cities* prepared for the Municipal
Manpower Commission by Donald C. Stone and Robert L. Brown, Graduate School of Public and International Affairs, University of Pittsburgh. It
is a handbook for students, teachers, personnel officers, vocational coun-
selors, and others concerned with urban public service.

service, especially in the more advanced administrative and functional fields, will have many opportunities for employment.

Chart 14 illustrates the several directions a career in urban affairs may take. Top level professional persons can move easily from government into community organizations, universities, and business firms that need a competent person in the urban field. The student learns early in his career of the diversity of organizations which are linked together in serving an urban area.

Educational Requirements for Urban Service

Some persons with only a high school or junior college diploma enter municipal service at lower levels and advance on the basis of demonstrated merit. However, they are at a disadvantage when competing with college and professional school graduates. Many positions, especially those with higher educational requirements, are closed to them entirely. With few exceptions, the completion of four years at a college or university is a *minimum* requirement.

Increasingly, for top administrative and staff positions, a master's or professional school degree is a desirable requirement. The person who has completed standard preparation in public administration, business management, finance, city planning, public health, social work, and other professional fields will have the advantage of securing better positions in terms of pay and of opportunities for rapid advancement, even if a special degree is not mandatory.

CHART 14

Career Possibilities in Urban Affairs

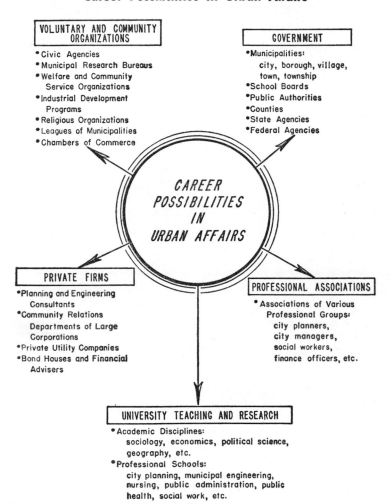

VOLUNTARY AND COMMUNITY ORGANIZATIONS
- Civic Agencies
- Municipal Research Bureaus
- Welfare and Community Service Organizations
- Industrial Development Programs
- Religious Organizations
- Leagues of Municipalities
- Chambers of Commerce

GOVERNMENT
- Municipalities:
  city, borough, village, town, township
- School Boards
- Public Authorities
- Counties
- State Agencies
- Federal Agencies

CAREER POSSIBILITIES IN URBAN AFFAIRS

PRIVATE FIRMS
- Planning and Engineering Consultants
- Community Relations Departments of Large Corporations
- Private Utility Companies
- Bond Houses and Financial Advisers

PROFESSIONAL ASSOCIATIONS
- Associations of Various Professional Groups:
  city planners,
  city managers,
  social workers,
  finance officers, etc.

UNIVERSITY TEACHING AND RESEARCH
- Academic Disciplines:
  sociology, economics, political science, geography, etc.
- Professional Schools:
  city planning, municipal engineering, nursing, public administration, public health, social work, etc.

Chart 15 indicates the number of years required to obtain such professional preparation.

Municipal governments recruit many specialists, technicians, and staff advisers from the science field: psychologists, biologists, chemists, physicists, sociologists, and economists.

CHART 15

Years of Education Required in 11 Professional Fields

Field	College Education (years)	Professional Curriculum (years)
Medicine	4	4
Dentistry	3	3
Hospital Administration	4	2*
Law	4	3
Social work	4	2 to 4*
Architecture	1–3	3 to 4
Library science	4	1
Public health	4	1 to 3*
Public Administration	4	1 to 2*
City planning	4	2*
Engineering	1–3	2–4

* Masters and professional degrees in these fields often follow other professional degrees.

From the professional schools, they draw engineers, planners, city managers, hospital administrators, health directors, and others. There are two generally accepted ways to obtain the basic education and training in these specializations: (1) to earn a degree in the social, physical, or biological sciences; (2) to graduate from a professional school. The aim of professional schools is to develop the intellectual comprehension, the practical skill, and the professional attitudes a member of the profession must acquire. The school also serves to bring employment opportunities to the attention of its students and aid them in finding their first jobs.

Career Opportunities in Selected Fields

A general knowledge about the opportunities in municipal service and the preparation required is essential for the person with a serious interest in a career in this field. Hence, the most distinctive and important professional fields are described in the following pages. This description includes the kinds of activities involved, career opportunities and education requirements.

Chief Executives

At the center of a modernized municipality is an appointed professional chief administrator selected by and responsible to its elective officials. Increasingly, the chief administrator is selected on the basis of his qualifications for the position, rather than on his political affiliation or place of residence. He is known as city manager, borough manager, general manager, executive director, chief administrative officer, or city administrator.

County governments are also undergoing modernization, particularly in the rapidly expanding metropolitan areas. County administrators and managers are beginning to replace the diffused and ineffective arrangement of multiple-headed administration.

Becoming a city or county administrator begins with

appointment as a junior assistant or intern. These positions provide an effective bridge between graduate programs in public administration and general management responsibility in cities and public authorities. The beginning positions carry many titles: administrative assistant, budget analyst, staff assistant, and administrative aide.

A graduate with a master's degree in municipal or public administration may start his career as an assistant in the office of a city manager or other top administrator. Increased responsibilities come quickly, and advancement is usually rapid. The young assistant is often assigned to budget, personnel, or administrative improvement tasks. If he shows real talent, he can move in a period of five or six years into middle-management level or become the city manager of a small municipality. From that position he may move to a larger city. Once his reputation is established, he has a number of choices in government at all levels, in business, or in education. For those qualified and inclined, there are overseas assignments under government and private sponsorship.

Special attention is directed to the "public authority" and "special district," new types of agencies which have emerged in local government in recent years. A considerable number of these special bodies have been established in most urban areas to administer such important functions as transportation, airports, housing, sanitation, water supply, and port operations. These authorities generally employ experienced chief executives and functional administrators for top positions. There are over 3,000 such agencies in our 212 metropolitan areas. Chart 16 lists some of the more common types.

CHART 16

Typical Agencies and Departments in Local Government

Operating Departments

Buildings	Public Health
Code Enforcement	Public Safety
Corrections	Public Welfare
Electric Power	Public Works
Fire	Recreation
Highways	Sanitation
Hospitals	Schools
Housing	Tax and Revenue
Library	Traffic Engineering
Licenses and Permits	Transportation
Parks	Urban Renewal
Police	Water

Staff Agencies

Budget	Municipal Research and Reference
City Clerk	Organization and Methods
City Planning	Personnel
Finance and Accounting	Public Information
Legal Counsel	

Public Authorities

Auditorium	Rivers and Drainage
Hospitals	Sewage
Housing	Schools
Industrial Development	Transit
Parking	Transportation
Parks	Urban Redevelopment
Port Development	Utilities
Public Buildings	Water

City Planning

Progressive governments of all except the smallest cities and of most urban counties have a city planning director and supporting professional staff. Urban renewal agencies, including redevelopment and housing authorities, require planners. Most state planning agencies are in the market for city planners with professional preparation, as are state planning boards and the Housing and Home Finance Agency. Planners are concerned with the economic, political, governmental, social, geographic, and physical aspects of communities; with the forces that influence their growth and development; and with the formulation and design of plans that will meet the needs of urban society.

A prime need of growing metropolitan regions is a strong planning agency. In the past few years, regional planning organizations—many on a voluntary basis—have come into being. These organizations provide opportunities for city planners to meet problems of greater dimensions.

The city planner has broad responsibilities for: arranging residential, commercial, and industrial parts of the city so that each part can perform its function with minimum cost and conflict; surroundings that are comfortable, convenient, and aesthetically pleasing; linking all parts of the city by an efficient system of transportation and communication; developing appropriate standards for lot size, sunlight, green space, and parking; promoting sanitary, safe, and comfortable housing; planning a high standard of recreation, schools, and other community services; planning adequate and economical water supply, sewerage, and other public programs.

While planning agencies employ architects, engineers,

urban economists, geographers, sociologists, political scientists, and public administrators, a person who wishes to move broadly into the city and regional planning field should enroll in a two-year graduate program at a recognized school of planning. A background in the social sciences, engineering, or architecture is generally preferred for entrance to these planning schools.

Finance and Accounting

Cities and other local governmental units employ a variety of technical and professional persons to carry out their tax collections, treasury, purchasing and supply, accounting, cost studies, auditing, investment, and other fiscal functions. A person can move into these positions immediately after completing his studies in business, economics, or public administration; or he can first secure experience in a public accounting firm or in a business finance office.

Finance directors are frequently selected from persons with accounting education and experience. Many finance directors also serve as budget officers and perform numerous other general administrative functions on behalf of the chief executive. In such cases, broad preparation in public or municipal administration is desirable.

With the growth of electronic data processing and its rapidly expanding use by governments, accountants will increasingly be involved in using an array of new quantitative methods. For a career as an accountant, a college degree with a major in accounting is a minimum. For students who

go on for a master's degree in business or public administration, higher levels of administrative responsibility will
be open to them in the finance field.

Urban Renewal, Redevelopment, and Housing

In many respects the most challenging work in the urban
field relates to the planning, renewal, and redevelopment
of cities. Faced with problems of shifts in population, obsolescence, blight, and decay, cities now are engaged in
strenuous efforts to rebuild and replan major parts of both
the central portion and outlying areas to make them suitable for modern living.

Most urban counties as well as cities now have urban
renewal departments or authorities. Their work is broadening to a concern with the total development of the city. In
mid-1962, renewal programs were under way in almost 600
cities.

Whatever the title of the organization, all require executive and program directors with a broad knowledge of problems faced by the modern city. They must have the capacity to mobilize a wide range of professional and technical
staffs to carry forward comprehensive development and redevelopment undertakings, advise policy makers, and inter-
pret these undertakings for the public.

These renewal, redevelopment, and housing agencies
employ planners, architects, engineers, economists, fiscal
experts, lawyers, social workers, recreation directors, hous-

ing managers, and many other kinds of professional and technical personnel.

Because of their recognized importance and rapid growth, these agencies offer unusually attractive work and career opportunities. There is also a need for the same kinds of personnel in state and federal urban renewal and housing agencies and in some of the voluntary and business organizations operating in this field.

College graduates in the social sciences or engineers who have undertaken a master's program in municipal or public administration are well qualified. Graduates of schools of business administration, social work, and law, or persons with other suitable professional or technical backgrounds who have engaged in advanced urban and management studies, will have a wide choice of jobs. If the same person has engaged in a graduate program in urban renewal and redevelopment administration, he will have a special advantage in being able to decide what city and what type of position he wishes to undertake. Those interested in citizen participation in urban renewal work can train in graduate programs in community organization and community work.

———•—•———

Public Works and Engineering

To the man in the street, the activities of public works departments are most evident. Whether the task is the construction of a bridge, excavation for a sewer line, the replacement of old lamp posts by mercury vapor or fluorescent lights, or the collection of refuse, everyone can note and watch what is being done. Virtually every city with a population of 5,000 or more has a public works or city engineering department.

Typical functions of municipal public works departments are the design, construction, and maintenance of streets, bridges, street lighting, sidewalks, and sewerage systems; regulation of street openings; design, installation, and maintenance of traffic signs and signals; surveying and map-making; maintenance of motor vehicles, public buildings, and off-street parking facilities; street cleaning, refuse collection, and disposal; administration of construction contracts; review of sub-division plans; building inspection; and the operation of sewage treatment facilities. Other functions entailing design, construction, operation, and maintenance which are often assigned to public works departments are parks, markets, docks, public buildings, cemeteries, parking meters, and airfields. Publicly operated utilities, which are discussed in the next section, are sometimes assigned to public works departments, particularly in the smaller cities.

Public works services offer a wide range of opportunity for persons with high aims for a professional or technical career. Engineers are in greatest demand, especially graduates in civil engineering, although mechanical, traffic, and electrical engineers are needed in considerable numbers. Engineers handle the major design, development, project, and operating responsibilities of public works departments.

In cities with populations of 10,000 to 15,000 or less, the public works director is often called the city engineer. In large cities, the engineering or design and construction division of the public works department may employ as many as 50 engineers.

Students who desire to enter the public works engineering field should select an engineering school which features courses in water supply, sanitation, refuse and sewage disposal, street design and construction, city planning, subdivision control, traffic engineering, and similar subjects. Some universities feature a combination of municipal engineering and municipal administration course work at the graduate level.

Public Utilities

City dwellers are vitally dependent upon organized systems, private or public, to supply electricity, water, gas, telephone, and other services.

Water. Most cities own and operate their own water facilities, including sources of supply, treatment and pumping plants, and storage and distribution systems. These essential systems, and those which are privately owned, must be planned and constructed well in advance of need and operated with great care. They must serve industry's as well as citizens' needs and also provide for sufficient fire protection.

Although the nation's water supply industry has established an outstanding record over the past fifty years in providing a safe product, it faces acute challenges. By 1980 the nation will need 600 billion gallons of water a day, twice as much as we use now. Meeting the urban and industrial demands will require large-scale planning, construction, and expenditures. The water supply industry must develop new sources of water, some that will require transporting water hundreds of miles. It must improve present methods and develop new methods of treatment, not only to increase the quality of its product, but also to treat polluted sources of water supply. To do all this, it needs skilled and energetic people in management and planning, design and construction, research, and operation.

Electricity. In 1958 there were 1,875 municipally owned electric utility systems, ranging in size from the very large Los Angeles system to those owned and operated by small towns. Publicly owned electric utility systems accounted for about 25 per cent of the total electric power distributed in the United States in 1959.

The municipally owned electric systems comprise one of the rapidly growing segments of the power industry. On the average, their power sales have been doubling every eight to nine years. There is a consequent steady growth in the responsibilities of the top utility management positions. Among the more important positions are those for general managers, electrical engineers, electricians, accountants, and persons with a variety of technical capacities.

Regulation. Although the primary responsibility for regulation of privately owned public utility companies rests in state and federal agencies, municipalities issue franchises and regulate public utility installations and operations. Lawyers, rate experts, appraisers, and engineers are required for these responsibilities.

Schools of business administration and engineering are the principal sources of education relating to public utilities regulation. A number of law schools give courses dealing with the legal aspects of public utility organization, rate making, and regulation. In some universities, the general policy issues relating to private versus public ownership, the social and economic aspects of utility services, and problems of rate making and enforcement are covered in the programs of the departments of political science, economics, or schools of public administration.

Transportation and Traffic Control

The development of efficient, convenient, and comfortable transportation is one of the major needs of American cities. Traffic congestion, financial problems of transit companies and commuter railroads, and the growing need for long-range solutions continually make headlines. Bold and imaginative approaches to urban transportation are required.

The elements of the problem are complex and will require a new generation of professional and technical personnel to cope with them. Shifts in population and changing patterns of movement within metropolitan areas have made street railway systems obsolete. In the absence of mass transit to accommodate the exploding population of the suburbs, more and more people have been forced to depend on their own automobiles, often a second car, for travel. As a result of increased costs and falling revenues, many suburban railroad commuting services have been curtailed or discontinued. These changes have pushed more and more automobiles on highways with increased congestion in the central city. At great cost, streets have been widened, throughways built, and buildings demolished for parking areas. And the end is not yet in sight.

There is in some areas, however, an awakened appreciation that the principal solution lies in greatly expanded mass transportation facilities. Express bus systems and, in some areas, rail rapid transit will be necessary to prevent stagnation and subsequent decay of cities. Urban transportation planning—a relatively new phrase—has become an essential in all large cities and metropolitan regions.

Up to the present time, only a few cities have engaged in comprehensive planning and established a concept of a comprehensive transportation system. But this situation will change rapidly as the problem grows increasingly acute and citizens accept the view that a planned system can provide the transportation service they expect and need. In large cities, this may mean the establishment of new or revitalized transit systems. Increasingly, municipalities will assume primary responsibility for transportation and establish public authorities to plan, organize, and operate the services. The federal government is recognizing that this is a national problem, and will provide leadership and funds.

With these developments will come attractive opportunities for professional service for persons with the right background: planners, transit specialists, engineers, traffic analysts, economists, accountants, transportation administrators, lawyers, appraisers, and related technical and professional persons. Salaries for professionally qualified persons will be especially favorable. Since the demand will far exceed supply, a talented person who secures advanced education for work in this field will have a wide choice of work opportunities.

Traffic Engineer. Special attention is directed to the traffic engineering profession, which is growing increasingly important as demands for throughways, by-passes, streets, and related motor vehicle services multiply. Traffic engineers are needed to plan, design, and supervise transportation complexes and such highway and city traffic devices as electronic traffic control systems. In addition, such persons are in great demand to plan new traffic patterns for developing and expanding neighborhoods and communities, both in urban core areas and in the suburbs.

———— • • ————

Legal Services

Cities encounter a wide range of legal problems; legislation must be interpreted to administrative and elective officials; ordinances must be drafted; legal issues in planning, zoning, land acquisition, and leasing must be analyzed and documents drafted. Utility regulation and the enforcement of laws and ordinances involve legal actions.

Cases must be prosecuted and judicial decisions implemented and enforced.

Municipal law is a broad and interesting field. Because attorneys play a significant role in counseling political leaders and administrative heads, many municipal law officers continue to serve for years in their posts even though they could earn far higher income from private practice or on the staff of business corporations.

Municipal attorneys are recruited from the law schools to fill junior positions. A competent lawyer with several years of municipal experience becomes a great asset to his city. Because of this experience, his services are often in demand by business corporations, law firms, and by state and national agencies. He can advance to the top law post as city solicitor or become a general counsel. In medium-sized and small communities, the city attorney is frequently retained on a part-time basis, so that he can carry on his private law practice at the same time.

Law Enforcement and Public Safety

Municipalities administer a considerable range of functions in law enforcement and public safety. In this area of responsibility are police and fire functions, building regulation and code enforcement, prosecution of offenders, prevention of crime and delinquency, probation, corrections, custody and care of minor offenders, clinics, and judicial administration.

Several categories of professional personnel are involved

in these activities. The law student who has an interest in public service will find varied opportunities in law enforcement. Prosecutors, legal defenders, and judges first must be admitted to the bar and qualify as lawyers. Often those who move into these posts are lawyers who have served with law firms and with other public jurisdictions. Persons interested in crime prevention or in work with juvenile offenders and youth boards may enter this field through a school of social work. Participation in civic activities often provides a good bridge into law enforcement work and other legal services.

Police administration is being rapidly professionalized. While most chiefs of police and other senior officers are promoted from within the ranks, there is a noticeable movement of professional police administrators from one jurisdiction to another. Moreover, progressive police departments systematically select a number of college graduates with a view to their moving into the more technical and responsible positions.

Somewhat the same situation exists in connection with fire administration, although here there is a greater tendency to promote the principal officers, including fire chiefs, from within the service.

Public Health and Hospital Administration

One of the most socially beneficial and rapidly growing professional fields is that of public health. With more than two-thirds of the nation's population now living in urban centers, local administration becomes the focus of health work. Traditionally, cities have been responsible for public health services. However, epidemics and germs do not respect political boundaries, and the trend is now to develop public health services on a county or metropolitan basis.

The emphasis, moreover, in public health work has shifted from measures for the control of epidemics and treatment of historical scourges to area programs stressing preventive medicine, sanitation, prevention of air and water pollution, medical care in the home, mental health, and problems of the chronically ill.

The principal professional staffs of public health departments include administrators, microbiologists, statisticians, sanitary engineers, physicians, dentists, nurses, medical social workers, nutritionists, and other specialists.

A critical shortage exists in all of these categories. It is especially acute in respect to public health administrators. Most graduates of public health schools specialize in such fields as microbiology, epidemiology, environmental sanitation, and veterinary public health. Only a handful focus on administration of public health departments. Meanwhile, over 1,000 full-time professional public health personnel are employed throughout the country in major administrative and management posts. Students who combine public health and administrative studies have exceptional career opportunities.

The college graduate with leadership potential who is interested in combining service in the public health field with administrative responsibilities can find a good outlet in hospital administration. Increasingly, hospitals are turning to professional administrators rather than to physicians to serve as superintendents and managers. The career channels are clear-cut. A graduate from a school or program in hospital administration is placed in a junior administrative position in a hospital, often on the staff of the manager. Here he is in a strategic position to learn about the total operation of a hospital and to advance up the career ladder. Movement to higher positions in other hospitals is a common practice, more so than in most other fields. The hospital administration market is a national market.

Public Welfare and Community Social Work

Public welfare is one of the most rapidly growing functions of local government. As is the case with public health, the financing and administration of public welfare programs entail federal, state, and local participation. Since the passage of the federal Social Security Act, every county in the United States has an office which administers public assistance programs, such as Old Age Assistance, Aid to Dependent Children, Aid to the Blind, and, in some states, a disability assistance program. (These programs are not to be confused with the social insurance programs to the aged, widows and children or "survivors" of deceased working citizens, and disabled persons, which are administered entirely by the federal government.)

Many, but not all, local agencies also administer public child welfare programs, including protective and placement services for children; specialized services to handicapped children; family casework services; indigent care, including medical assistance programs for the needy; delinquency prevention measures; clinical and probationary services; custodial and correctional institutions; licensing functions for institutions such as foster homes, day care facilities, and homes for the aged; various kinds of recreational and leisure time activities; vocational and counseling services; personal and budget adjustment services; and emergency measures, such as work relief programs and distribution of surplus commodities.

Voluntary social welfare agencies in the community provide additional important services and work cooperatively with the state and local departments of public welfare. In some cities specific welfare services are performed by private social welfare agencies; in other cities, by public welfare agencies. The trend generally in public welfare programs is to vest the welfare functions within a county-wide agency rather than in a municipal government office.

Public welfare departments employ a wide variety of professional personnel. Since the main core of their job is social work, they employ the various specialists within that field, such as social caseworkers, social group workers, community organization workers, and researchers. Public welfare departments also employ home economists, psychologists, attorneys, accountants, sociologists, psychiatrists, physicians, and other medical personnel, such as orthopedic nurses and ophthalmologists. Agency administrators have often risen in the field from one of the specialities after considerable experience. Persons who have engaged in advanced study in public welfare administration and occupied general program and administrative rather than technical posts are generally favored.

Graduate education in social work is the principal channel for entrance into professional responsibilities relating to welfare services. For beginning positions, a minimum of a bachelor's degree in the social sciences or the humanities is preferred. For advanced positions, graduate education is almost universally mandatory. Generally the same principle applies to persons who wish to fill posts as vocational rehabilitation experts, probation and parole officers, and child placement workers. Graduate work in psychology is required for clinical psychologists and quite frequently for psychometricians.

Public Recreation

Until recent times, city parks and open spaces were designed with the main purpose of creating "the city beautiful." With increased leisure time, the need for recreational facilities for all age groups has become a primary consideration. Public recreation departments have been set up in many cities to make effective use of playgrounds, parks, and other recreational facilities.

Recreation programs require planning, administration, counseling, and group leadership. For the person who enjoys working with people, recreation leadership and counseling offer satisfying opportunities. Moreover, the increasing life span of Americans presents a challenge to our society to provide recreation activities for the aged and retired. Almost 10 per cent of our population is 65 years or older.

Persons who possess professional preparation for recreation and youth leadership are in great demand both by public recreation agencies and by such voluntary agencies as the YMCA, YWCA, YMHA, Boy and Girl Scouts, Boys' and Girls' clubs, settlement houses, and community centers.

About 50 per cent of the full-time, year-round positions in public recreation are at the executive and supervisory level. Many of the students with graduate degrees skip the activities level entirely and move directly from school into positions of supervisory responsibility.

The recreation administrator must be qualified in all phases of administration: program planning, budgeting, costs accounting, supervision, construction, operation and maintenance, public administration, and public relations. In this sense, the administrative responsibilities of the head of a public recreation department are similar to those of other department directors.

Approximately 65 colleges and universities have established professional educational programs to train young men and women for recreation service. Some of these cover only the basic knowledge enabling one to serve as a director of a playground or counselor of an interest group. Many of the offerings form an integral part of physical education programs. A few institutions have developed a comprehensive curriculum in which program planning, organization, and management of recreational agencies are provided, as well as a solid grounding in human growth and behavior, counseling and guidance, group work, and intergroup relations. Specialization in group work in a school of social work is also excellent preparation. Such training emphasizes work with small groups in various informal education and leisure time activities rather than mass recreation, although planning broad recreation programs is included.

Park Development and Management

Open spaces and park development programs are two of the most pressing needs in urban areas today. The park director and his staff are concerned with promotion, development, and utilization of public parks and open land.

The top-level park administrator or specialist must have basic knowledge in five subjects: landscape architecture, horticulture, business administration, recreation, and design and construction. He also must be able to present the "case for parks" to the public.

There is a need for park managers, directors, planners, and specialists in every school district and at all levels of local government: municipal, county, and regional. In the medium-sized communities the trend is for park and recreation programs to be combined under one departmental director, who reports to the city manager or other chief administrative officer.

Standards for park personnel have risen tremendously in the past ten years. In nearly every case, the director is required to have a college education. If the director is specialized in one field, such as landscape architecture, then he has probably supplemented his background with considerable practical experience before becoming director.

Library Service

Municipal, county, and regional libraries have paralleled the growth of other educational institutions in contributing to a cultured and democratic nation. During the past century, librarianship has evolved from a mere custodial function to an applied science providing educational and technical services to all members of the urban community.

Librarianship requires a graduate degree in a school accredited by the American Library Association. In 24 states, librarians must be certified by a state licensing agency prior to employment with local public libraries. There are 36 accredited library schools in the United States.

Library schools and associations stress a nationwide demand for well-qualified librarians to serve the 7,900 public libraries. There is a specific need for librarians who offer marked aptitude for administration, social understandings of the changing urban community, and a sound knowledge of subject matter. Severe shortages exist in the fields of cataloging and work with children and young adults.

Despite the scarcity of staff, cities have been compelled to build additional branch libraries to take care of new housing developments. Regional libraries have demanded new buildings. The obsolescence of many central libraries has led to their replacement. The Library Services Act of the federal government and state attention to libraries have stimulated still greater efforts in public library expansion.

————•—•————

Municipal Research and Extension

Bureaus of municipal research, taxpayers' associations, university municipal research institutes, and the rapidly developing municipal extension services of state governments and universities are in urgent need of candidates who have had graduate preparation in municipal and public administration. The work of these organizations entails the study of municipal organization, management, and methods; and in addition, a wide range of metropolitan and intergovernmental financial and economic facility and service problems. Some focus largely on neighborhood improvement.

Young men or women with a good social science background or a degree in engineering, law, or business administration who secure graduate preparation for municipal research work will find their services in great demand. Their problem will be how to choose among a number of attractive openings. Career opportunities are especially favorable because the individual who has developed a reputation in this field can move freely among positions in municipal governments, private or voluntary municipal research agencies (which exist in most large cities), universities, and business corporations.

————•—•————

Instruction and Research in Universities

The education of persons for all of the foregoing fields of service will require an increasing number of university instructors. Many persons find satisfaction in "mobile" careers in which they move between public positions and university appointments, or to a research agency. Officials with suitable educational background are sought by universities to serve as part-time lecturers. Faculty members of universities often engage in municipal consulting and research work.

Many university programs are designed for the preparation of university teachers. This is especially true of students who major in the urban aspects of political science, economics, sociology, and geography. In each of these disciplines, at least a dozen universities have outstanding offerings.

Consulting Agencies to Municipal Governments

Increasingly, cities have been turning to consulting agencies for services of a specialized nature on a temporary or stand-by basis. Qualified consulting firms are available for advice and assistance in the fields of city planning, urban renewal, municipal engineering projects, bond and financial matters, auditing, revision of codes and city ordinances, personnel studies, and reorganizations and management surveys.

Many of these firms are operated by private individuals

and firms for profit. Others are financed by public contributions and engage on a cost basis in research, advisory, and consulting activities for public agencies in the area.

The directors and staff members of these firms and organizations frequently obtained their initial training and experience by serving in government or universities in the urban affairs field. After gaining this experience, they moved to the consulting field. There will continue to be a great demand for competent persons by consulting agencies. In addition to on-the-job experience, the interested person should develop a talent for writing, research, and analysis in his specialized field of interest. The consulting business will undoubtedly hold an attraction for many of the most competent persons in urban affairs work.

The Satisfactions of Municipal Service

Municipal service is not just one profession; it is many. For excitement and satisfaction, there are few professions comparable to that of a public career. Government has need of every professional and occupational skill—journalists, economists, educators, planners, lawyers, social workers, engineers, business experts, health officers, accountants, chemists, administrators, and many others.

Two elements are essential in municipal service. One is knowledge of the problems of urban society and urban services. The other is competence in management—of planning, coordination, and motivation of human effort.

The social, economic, political, geographical, administrative, and ethical aspects of urban life and development must be understood if communities are to be improved as suitable places in which to live and work.

At the higher administrative and program levels and in such fields as public health, public welfare, education, and law enforcement, the municipal official is dealing with the most intriguing and significant problems in modern society; problems whose diversity, complexity, and significance demand the highest degree of dedication and community service characteristic of the modern public servant.

If our cities are to be made and kept livable, good government must lead the way and take the primary responsibility. The kinds of policies, the level of services, and the caliber of local leadership will be reflected in the kind of young people attracted to positions in this field. The communities of America and the nation as a whole cannot afford anything less than the highest talent to assume responsibility for the tasks ahead.

Index